# Dream Makers —
## Stories That Won't Put You To Sleep

# Dream Makers

## An Anthology

by Authors of
The Writers Roundtable

Compiled by Val Dumond

**Muddy Puddle Press**
**Lakewood, Washington**

Edited by Val Dumond
Cover by SandsCostner & Associates
Cover photograph by Dan Sloan

ISBN 0-9679704-3-1

Printed in the United States of America

Muddy Puddle Press
P. O. Box 97124
Lakewood, WA 98497

# Table of Contents

### Dreamy/Romance and Adventure 129

## Pipe Dreams/Humor 161

# A Writer's Life

A writer's life is lonely, or so some say. A writer sits at a computer (typewriter, yellow pad, scribbling board) and waits for the words to come. At the end of a session, the writer wonders if there's anything on the paper that is worth letting other people read. Ah, poor writer, all alone!

No way!

Let me share a writer's secret: writing is one of the most exciting, stimulating, exhilarating, zestful, enjoyable, invigorating, fascinating activities anyone can find to do. As writers, we get to meet the most engaging characters (we dream them up), and we get to wield the godlike hand of fate to their comings and goings. We can obliterate them, raise them to new heights, make them adorable or hated, give them tics and idiosyncrasies, manipulate their relationships, soothe their anger or fire it up…oh, we can make our characters do anything we want.

Here's another writer's secret: we can't be lonely when we're surrounded by these wild and crazy "people." Sometimes we fall in love with our characters, or at least in admiration of them. And sometimes we learn to hate them (that's when we would like to obliterate them). If we like them and they are hateful, we get to improve their attitudes. You'd be surprised how many writers take great delight in turning villains into sweet loveable characters, and the other way around. That's drama!

The works you read in this anthology, all written by members of the Writers Roundtable, demonstrate all the elements of the writing process. Look for the villain who becomes a hero, the hero who falls — flat — along with the strange encounters and couplings of characters much like the people next door (maybe you need to move).

Originally, this book was planned to be a collection of grisly tales — nightmares. Then we learned that other kinds of stories can also keep you awake — so we added some fantasy, some inspiration, nostalgia, romance and adventure — dreamy tales. You'll also find stories that children will enjoy, and poetry — lots of poetry.

Notice the names of the authors. Notice how certain authors write in a variety of themes (we call them genres). Some of these writers have published other works and some are appearing in print for the first time. Check out their backgrounds in the Biography Section at the back of the book.

Notice the illustrations: some artists both write and draw. Their work is noted in the Acknowledgement Section. The separation illustrations were drawn by a member of the Writers Roundtable (she is a writer, poet *and* artist).

A lonely life? We don't think so. Most of us have "day jobs" and write when others have gone to bed, and some just write when the spirit moves us, but everyone — every last one — of us writes because we feel the need to get the words out and share our inspirations. And every last one of us dreams of the time we can spend all day writing.

Enjoy reading what these Dream Makers have written for you.

Val Dumond
Facilitator,
Writers Roundtable

# Making Dreams
## Charlotte Richards

"To sleep: perchance to dream," so said
The often-quoted bard,
But in these pages dreams hold sway
And peaceful sleep is barred.

For who can doze when evil grabs
The reader by the throat
In tales of rampant wickedness
Where villains plot and gloat?

Or horror lays its heavy hand
Upon our sweaty brow
And takes us on a journey far
Beyond the here and now?

Still other tales that make us grin
Will keep us wide awake,
For when we're laughing heartily,
A yawn is hard to fake.

Here, too, are poems that inspire.
They take us by the hand
And help us travel past our woes
Into some promised land.

Read on for flights of fantasy,
Romantic interludes,
Adventures and suspenseful tales
Evoking many moods.

Enjoy each page! You'll never nod.
Reality's not what it seems,
For every storyteller here
Is skilled at making dreams.

# Nightmares

...Between the acting of a dreadful thing
And the first motion, all the interim is
Like a phantasma, or a hideous dream...
—Shakespeare

THOMAS J. MARTIN

# When I Talk

I sat on the floor. I ate my graham cracker and said nothing. Miss
Richards sat on the couch bossing us kids at the day care
around. Sometimes it was better I said nothing, even when
things were not fair.

Miss Richards told Amy to get her a soda from the fridge. She'd
yell at us to keep quiet and she'd turn the channel from Disney and
Nickelodeon to her soaps. She'd pull her cigarettes and lighter from
her belt pouch and sit there until Mommy picked us up or she went
to use the bathroom. She'd let the little ones have stinky diapers.
She'd not hand out the snack.

Miss Richards was mean. When Mrs. Anderson left after lunch,
Miss Richards came in. She lived next door to the day care, down
the street from Mommy's house. She took toys from the kids and put
them on the top shelf just to be mean. She yelled at Cassandra and
made her cry. She made Amy, my sister, cry.

I did not say anything about Miss Richards to Mommy anymore.
When I asked Mommy why she had to work somewhere else and pay
someone to act as a mommy who was not nice, she cried. When
Mommy cries it is sadder than when Amy cries.

All the kids hated Miss Richards except Andy.

Andy does not hate no one. Andy is different. He has special
needs. He is much older than me but he does not talk at all. He
can't read. Andy scared me when he first came to day care because
he laughs at the wrong times on shows and he eats messy. He's much
bigger than the other kids but acts like the babies.

I liked Andy later because he listened when I read to Amy and
Cassie.

Andy also could get toys down from the top shelf. When Miss Richards took a toy and put it on the top shelf, I'd sometimes wait until she left the playroom and then point to something the same color as the toy, then at the shelf. Andy would get it down. The other kids liked Andy. They'd say, "Hi, Andy," when his mother dropped him off."

He'd smile. His mommy would be happy then.

One day something bad happened. Miss Richards took Amy's play phone because Amy and Cassie were playing phones too loud. When Miss Richards left the room, I pointed to the phones on the top shelf. Miss Richards came back and saw Andy give the phone to me. She hit him hard on the back of his head. He started screaming and would not stop. Andy's mommy picked him up. Miss Richards said Andy fell and hit his head. She lied. This was not fair.

That day Mommy picked us up. We ate dinner — hamburgers and fries. I watched TV with Mommy. Mike, Cassandra's older brother, was sitting on the porch wall in front near Cassie and Amy. I don't like Mike. He stole Mommy's CD player from the porch. She used to sing and do a funny dance. Mommy does not let us talk to Mike. She says he smokes crack. I did not want to talk to Mike. He sat on the wall looking at me when I came outside.

I told Amy and Cassie I saw a man with a lot of money on TV. I said Miss Richards had more money in her pouch on her tummy than the man on TV. Amy said she did not care. I did not care she did not care. I went back in to watch TV with Mommy.

Mike left.

When we got to the day care the next morning, I saw police cars in front of Miss Richards' house. Yellow tape was in front of the house like on Cops.

Mommy talked to Mrs. Anderson. Mrs. Anderson acted funny. Mommy told us kids that Miss Richards was not coming back to the day care. Mrs. Anderson asked Mommy to work for her since Miss Richards was gone. Mommy said yes!

The DARE officer, Deputy Bennett, came over and talked to us. He did not talk about drugs this time. He said we should lock our doors always and know to call 911 if something bad happens. Then he asked us kids about Miss Richards.

I sat on the floor.

I ate my graham cracker and said nothing, *but I smiled.*

# The Heroes of New York

## Matthew A. Geraci

They saw fire in the sky.
People ran from this inferno
As one runs from evil in a nightmare.
Though this heart ran into it,
Even into its belly they ran,
These had no fear.
For they ran for no prize,
Nor for any reward.
For this they ran.
A reward that is not seen.
For if this man was to see,
He would think, "Not I."
Though this he thought not.
For he moved not with his knowledge.
For all his wisdom would have said,
"I could be no more if I was to enter this place."
For not one of those moved that day.
For look and see, they moved not.
Though moved they were,
Not once, three times,
The cement fell upon them;
They did not waiver.
Again the cement fell;
They did not waiver.
Again the cement cracked and steel broke;
They did not run.
How is this, that a man can do such a thing?
To run into the belly of death.
Knowing his brothers have been swallowed?
This I do not know.
Though this I do.
He serves with what he sees with.
That is, he serves with his heart.
Therefore, those brothers before him and above him say,
"Well done, you have served and paid so others may live."
Amen

JAMES FRANCIS SMITH

# Gamel and Mrs. O'Malley

J ust minutes after Nora O'Malley emerged from the nearby subway entrance, a frowning Gamel entered the skyscraper's swiftly revolving door and scurried across the lobby. The frown lengthened when he recalled his old Harvard buddy's New England accent and his all-too-familiar greeting,

"Hey Camel Driver, we plan to be in the Big Apple this weekend. Use your influence to acquire some theater tickets. You and Lois are welcome to tag along. Remember it was my idea. Therefore, Meredith and I are entitled to the best seats." Little did Gamel realize that the confident Prescott Jones the Fourth would become his only American friend. Being a token foreign companion didn't bother Gamel; however, being used as a ticket procurer without adequate notice gnawed at his faltering self-confidence.

Gamel jostled his way through the crowd and headed toward the bank of elevators marked floors fifty-one to one-hundred five. On most mornings, he used this time to enjoy all that Allah had provided. The seven o'clock beeping of his watch made him aware that he missed the Muslim sunrise prayer. Instead of meditating as he neared the elevator, he turned his attention toward another day of managing irritable employees. Why should he care that many were jealous of his swift advancement? He was eternally grateful for Prescott's solid advice when they discussed the subject of jealous employees.

"Take their prejudice as a compliment," Prescott said. "Rather than facing up to their own inadequacies, most people prefer to believe that others advance because of connections. Never pay attention to people in a lower status."

Replaying the conversation, Gamel realized that it's easier for a self-assured American to ignore slights than a kid from Cairo's slums.

As though on command, Nora O'Malley, his executive assistant, squeezed next to him greeting him in her soft Killarney brogue with a cheerful, "Good morn'inn, Mr. Sifain."

The ritual of meeting near the elevator door was as old as their eight-year working relationship. Gamel wondered how she invariably muscled her way through those trying to board, timing her approach to meet him exactly as the door opened. Their seemly by-chance meetings began shortly after Nora confessed to being frightened on swift-moving elevators.

"My home in Ireland didn't have a second story, and I always used the stairs while attending Fordham University," she explained. "Knowing that someone as important as yourself rides the same elevator gives me a grand feeling of confidence."

In reply, Gamel confessed his own fear — the first time he mounted a camel, a fear that had become greatly magnified in this city of high rises. On a windy day, the entire office tower swayed a foot and a half. He received cold comfort from the building management's explanation that the movement added to the safety of the structure. In a feeble effort to integrate his religious beliefs with modern engineering, Gamel routinely squeezed the leather briefcase handle while quietly repeating the Quran's teaching, *And He has set firm mountains in the earth so that it would not shake with you.*

His and Nora's office mannerisms were, by necessity, quite formal. Their shared secret of fearing simple elevator rides, however, had created a bond that overshadowed their vast hierarchical differences within the organization. The interlude of the pair's pleasantries evaporated before they entered Jacobson Investment Firm's elaborate one-hundred-third-floor suite.

When he saw the yellow Post-It note on his executive desk pad, Gamel knew the day would be worse than most. He opened a locked cabinet drawer, retrieved the Saudi Petroleum contract and mentally composed the bid letter requiring Jacob Jacobson's signature. Just as he pressed the intercom to request that Mrs. O'Malley bring her steno pad, the building trembled as though hit by a violent gush of wind. Before he could utter the words, "what happened?" an ashen-faced Nora O'Malley appeared at his office door.

"May the Laard save us, Mr. Sifain. A big airplane crashed into the tower next door." Then Nora, who absorbed every floating office rumor, announced, "They say that people are falling to their deaths."

Swiftly leaving his office and racing to the windows on the other side of the building, Gamel shoved his way through the gathering crowd and looked in horror at the billowing inferno. Then he recited a long forgotten prayer to Allah before turning toward his terrified employees.

"Should we leave?" someone asked.

Gamel's cat-quick wit determined that precaution would be best served by keeping people near their workstations.

"Before anyone makes a mad dash, please listen to me. Thousands are already crowding the elevators and stairs. Furthermore, the streets will soon be flooded with ambulances, police cars and fire engines. We're not in any danger. We can leave in an orderly fashion once the hysteria has died down. Call your loved ones. Tell them you're safe. You might have a better chance of getting connected if you used a cell phone. If you don't have one, you are welcome to use mine."

Satisfied with his encouraging words, Gamel hurried to his office wondering if he should bother with the Saudi bid letter. Since work was furthermost from his mind, he decided to call Lois.

With Gamel well out of earshot, his disgruntled employees questioned his motives and particularly his national bias. Many, veterans of an earlier car bombing by Arab fundamentalists, refused to believe that the plane crash happened accidentally.

Unaware of the growing dissention, Gamel pulled out his executive chair when a blur outside the window caught his eye. "Allah have mercy," he said aloud, as he looked in horror at the oncoming jetliner. The enormity of watching a second plane come screaming toward him momentarily shut down the reasoning side of his brain. Instead of taking cover, he just stared out the window.

The building shuddered. The executive chair rolled across the floor, flung Gamel against the far wall and then abruptly dumped him. He lay gasping for air when a bleeding Mrs. O'Malley half-crawled through the office doorway and asked if he was all right.

"Did you see it?" he asked dumbfounded. "A plane crashed into this building somewhere below us. Let's see if anyone is hurt and then see if we can get out of here."

The look of shock on Nora's face made Gamel immediately sorry that he used the word *if*. "I mean *how* we can get out of here," he corrected himself. "Let me think for a minute."

A few moments passed before Gamel spoke again. "Since the plane struck this side of the building, the stairs at the far corner would be our best chance."

Racing from his office with Nora in tow, Gamel first inquired if anyone was severely injured. Finding none, he ordered everyone to follow him. The next words froze his heart as though he had been stabbed by a shard of ice.

"We're not following you anywhere," shouted a middle-aged, middle manager.

"If you hadn't stopped us, we would have been safely out of here," someone else yelled.

Pandemonium broke out; some ran toward the elevators while others headed for the stairs. Before long, most returned to the relative safety of their work area beaten back by intense heat and smoke that seeped through openings.

"When will the firemen get here?" a panicky voice cried out.

"Don't be a ninny," an angry reply came. "Ladders only reach to the seventh floor."

"We're all doomed because of that Arab," the middle-aged, middle manager shouted while searching for something to fling in Gamel's direction. Others vainly slammed chairs against the tempered plate glass windows. A feeling of entrapment pervaded as coats, shirts and even blouses were shed to gain a sense of relief from the heat. As the temperature rose so did fear and tempers.

Gamel, accompanied by his only ally, Mrs. O'Malley, retreated to his office and barred the door.

"What can we do?" Nora asked. Cold tears of despair streamed down her face.

"We can only pray," Gamel answered quietly. Then looking at his frightened administrative assistant, he said calmly, "Perhaps you should try calling your husband."

"I have little chance of reaching Barney now," she replied. "He's a fireman, you know."

Gamel felt a tinge of embarrassment for he had never inquired as to Nora's husband's name, let along his occupation. Gamel's mind turned quickly to Lois and the twins. He tried again to reach them but heard his own voice with its quirky message on the answering machine. After waiting for the beep, he told Lois of his love and pleaded that she raise their children with dignity. Then he handed the cell phone to Nora saying, "I think you should leave a message as well."

"Ah, Barney never believed in answering machines. He preferred to hear a human voice." Nora leaned her blood-caked forehead against the office door. She opened her purse and extracted a pair of rosary beads saying, "I knew this lofty building would be the death of me. May our Laard have mercy on my soul."

Placing his arm around her shoulder, Gamel, perhaps for the first time, thanked his faithful assistant for her years of loyal service. "Jaysus, Mary and Joseph, "she screamed. "My shoes are dissolving from the heat." The two clamored onto the executive desk to escape the white heat radiating from the inferno below. Holding onto Nora for balance, Gamel confessed, "I am more afraid of fire than I am of heights."

Panicked by his employees' growing hatred and terrified of a firey death, he leaped from the desk, flung open the door and hurried toward the closest bank of elevators. Using his bare hands, he wedged open the glowing hot doors. Hopelessness turned his thoughts to Islam. Ignoring his pain, Nora's presence and the gaping of his employees, he raised blistered hands to his ears and prayed, "Allah u Al-kabeer" (Allah is the greatest). When he finished the solemn ritual, he moved toward the open elevator shaft.

"Suicide is a mortal sin," a shoeless Nora said gravely as she caught up with Gamel. Then tightly gripping the rosary beads, she grabbed his arm and begged, "Gamel, please wait for me."

Neither Gamel nor Mrs. O'Malley felt Tower II crumble as they stepped off into space.

# United In Despair
## (In memory of Sept 11, 2001)

### JULIE JENNINGS

Gusting wind like child's play
Swirls a blaze of colors to the ground.
Resplendent as a tree of hope.

Brushed heartache of despair;
Deliberate force explodes.
Impact shocks
Thickets of injury and death.

Clear skyline crimson,
Like an ill-made Lego building;
Towers collapse.

Bruised hearts united
Brinked for battle.
Cascade of leaves
Bury the debris

Tainted in autumn's
   Treachery.

BARBARA J. WYATT

# Ain't No Alabama Hillbilly

With his arms draped over the handles of the wave runner, Andy felt drained yet at peace. He glanced back and saw the three bodies floating face down in the water.

A Yamaha wave runner, with its blue and purple padded seat, drifted alongside one body like a faithful hound dog. Its engine still warm, it coasted as it waited for the rider to remount, plug in a lanyard and start off for another loud fast cruise through the waters of Lake Martin. The two other bodies, also face down, were accompanied by their wave runners. One was a late model water bike that continued to drive around and around in small circles.

The arms of one body were spread wide in a V, like a black turkey vulture soaring in the blue sky looking for carrion. But this body floated silently on the surface of the water, dead.

*I kin get back to my lake house, park my machine, then call. First, need to wait till my engine cools. No. I'll call right 'way. I say: "I found the bodies, sir, and headed right home." "Why you didn't check if they were dead?" the cop will say. (Hmm. Hold on, let me think, let me think. I can cum up with somethin'. I ain't no Alabama hillbilly.)*

It did come.

*I know what'd I say: "I saw one man. He called me a hillbilly, a bird lovin' homosexual hillbilly. But I didn't do nothin'. I just headed off. He shoudn'ta said that, ya know. Didn't want no trouble. Then I saw the other two and they all hit each other. They's all dead, I figured. I could jist tell. Didn't have to touch 'em. Ain't no Alabama hillbilly, ya know. I figure'd I needed to call you right soon. So I called." There, that sounded good.*

Andy nodded, revved up his wave runner and headed toward home. He smiled and moved in rhythm with his machine. With a

13

slight turn to the right, he stood several inches off the seat and shifted his weight to his right leg. He increased the speed and created a large splash from the spin of the machine.

*Wait a minute*. He dropped his smile, removed his finger from the power button and coasted. *That don' make no sense. They'd ask me, "Whacha' doing when they'd crash? How'd you'd know they crash?" the cop will say. I gotta cum up with an answer. Cain't be no Alabama hillbilly*.

Andy coasted for a few minutes. He heard a loud "kweeer" and looked over to the woods for the red head of one of the lake's many woodpeckers. He could hear it pecking against a tree. He was scanning the large grouping of trees by the shore when his concentration was broken by the loud roar of a wave runner off on his right.

Andy raised his hand in the Lake Martin straight-arm palm-open wave salute and the man responded in a like manner.

*Should I stop him? No. Let him go on, let him go on*. He watched the wave runner speed by. Andy's machine rose and dipped in the residual waves.

*I gotta think. I gotta cum up with a' answer. What was I doin' when they crashed? Why didn't I check 'em?*

He turned his head and watched the other wave runner disappear down the lake. *I shouldn'ta let him by. I shouldn'ta let him go by! He's going to find the bodies before I cum up with my answer. Before I call. Wait, maybe he won't.*

Andy concentrated on the man's back as he disappeared around the next bend. He waited. Then he heard it. The engine slowed down.

*Gotta git there*. Andy turned his wave runner back on and spun to the left, all but tipping over the machine. *I gotta catch him. Gotta git there quick.*

Andy crouched down with his eyes mere inches above the handles of the machine. *This'll help me go faster, create windflow. Com'on, faster, baby. Com'on.* He rounded the bend and saw the man was close to one of the bodies and its wave runner.

*He's seen 'em! I know'd he'd seen the bodies. Just like da other two.*

"Hey there. You okay?" Andy heard him yell at the bodies. The man drove closer to one of the floating bodies and stopped. He lifted an arm and struggled to pull the body onto his machine. He turned and saw Andy. He extended his arm and waved Andy over. It wasn't the Lake Martin salute. It was the universal sign for "come and help."

14

Andy headed toward the man. He reduced his speed and lined up his machine. He opened the engine full throttle and propelled his machine toward the man and the body. His machine leaped up over a small residue wake and slammed into the man. The body splashed back into the lake. The man screamed as he soared over it and landed head first in the water. Andy maneuvered a turn between two floating wave runners.

When the man's head popped up on the surface, Andy powered up and drove through the man's face. He felt a thud under his feet. He cut the engine and listened. *I don't want to look. But I gotta. Let me just think first.*

He coasted and listened to the quiet rattling of the beak of a red-headed woodpecker against a tree. *I ain't no Alabama hillbilly. I can figure this out. I'll go to the police and tell them I found the bodies. They musta' hit each other. That's it. They musta all hit each other. I didn't see nothin'.*

He glanced behind to see the fourth body face down in the water. Its wave runner floated close by. He closed his eyes. *I sure don't like this. But it's over. I'll get back and call the police.* "Jist been an accident at Lake Martin. Come quick."

Once more with his arms draped over the handles of his wave runner, Andy felt drained, yet at peace on that stifling Alabama summer day.

He heard a "chewink, chewink." *I know that bird. That's a Pipilo erthrophthalumus A Towbee.*

Then he heard a second sound. Another wave runner was approaching.

NADINE McKEE

# Paper Balloons

I f I could uncross my feet I could perhaps understand what is happening to me. Has the Medic-1 ambulance responding to my 911 emergency call crashed on the way to St. Joseph's Hospital? Where am I? I no longer feel severe crushing chest pains. I cannot use my right arm. It is tightly secured. My breathing is easier. What is wrong? Have I been given a wrong anesthetic or an experimental drug? There are voices around me I cannot hear and movements I cannot see. I can no longer hear the wailing sirens of Medic-1.

My feet are so heavy. Why can't I uncross me feet? I want to march — left, right, left, right....

Out of a nothing atmosphere I sense my daughter standing at the right side of my hospital bed, yet she is in a far-off hazy fog. She is gone, then she is again at my bedside. In the light soft reflection of the full moon I know tears from her Norwegian blue eyes spill down her cheeks. She is holding my hand. Why is she here? I try to hold her small hand protecting her from her childhood fears, but I have no strength. I cannot feel the warmth of her hands. In drifting clouds I hear her voice that is full of tears saying, "Mom. I love you, Mom," but I cannot see or hear her words of anguish. She is a grown woman now, holding my hand, protecting me. Why?

In the quiet of the same moonlight I hear my son's deep voice pleading with me, but I cannot see him. "Come back, Mom, come back," he keeps calling softly. He strokes my hand as if I am a sleeping kitten, yet I cannot feel his hands. I cannot see the tears in his blue, blue eyes but I can hear the pain of his silent voice. His childhood laughter is gone. Why is he calling out to me? I am right here beside him. Disarray reigns through my musing.

From a milky shadow, my dead mother calls me, "Dean! Nadine!" Startled, I try to sit up as I often did when Mother called to me in the dreams of my childhood. Slowly the light disappears and her voice fades like an echo that does not answer from a distant mountain. She does not call to me — ever again.

I am confused by the voices I cannot hear, and my feet are so very heavy. I feel the cold air that holds me, yet there are no restraints binding me. My meandering thoughts are often my only companions. Time is like paper balloons playing in the gentle breeze of my days and nights. I am alone with familiar sounds I cannot hear or see.

I am cold again. Slowly an expanse of tranquil distant silky white light gathers in a far-off sky. My eyes are not open, yet I see this glorious wonder. Like a great fan of welcome, a new calmness moves close to me. The cone-shaped expanse of light creeps to the edge of my vision, and all fear vanishes.

Am I dying? This is gracious death? I cannot move away from my grating chest pains, yet they slip away. The magnificent beacon that encompasses everything about me comforts me. If this is death, let it take me. I am not afraid.

Then, I become angry because death will not take me. Death will not let me rest. Warm hands hold mine.

The compassion and depth of the soft light again linger ever so close to me. The light does not touch me. Like a slow waltz without music it rolls away, then back again, shuddering as it welcomes me into the comfort of its waning light. I do not struggle. Then, as soft and peacefully as this restful light appears, it slowly slips away.

My feet are so heavy. Why can't I uncross my ankles? I am warm again. A small hand is holding mine, gently. Tears are in words that I cannot hear. Asking, pleading, gaunt words are again and again begging, "Mom. Come back, Mom. We love you."

The pretty paper balloons of time again dance away my confusion. I know — I think I know — my son Oscar and my daughter Barbara are near me. I feel their presence, yet I cannot see them. I have no eyes. I have no ears. I have no voice. My love for my family is my only strength. Our strong family love holds my hands and my heart to keep me with them, just as their love pushes the same pretty balloons in and out of my weakened mind and body. I am very tired.

A powder-green glob fuzzes in and out of my illusions. Is this greenish moving light coming to welcome me, too? If this is God, he has short-cropped black hair and is smiling down at me. I sense I am in a hospital room and a real human being dressed in intensive-care greens is standing beside my bed.

"Good morning, Nadine," are his words. I can hear him! I can hear his voice very close to me. I feel his busy hands continually checking a tangled maze of lifeline tubes and large intravenous needles injected into my body.

I want to say, "Good morning," but the words in my brain will not make sounds. I know I can open my eyes. 1 can see this man in green. I can hear this man in green. I am not dead!

The voice of the man in green scrubs standing beside my bed suddenly becomes excited. "Merry Christmas, Nadine. Welcome back to our world." His greenish blur disappears from my sight as he calls out, "Jim! Jim! Call Nadine's family. Hurry! She smiled at me. Her eyes are open! She's awake!"

The Green Man returns to my bedside, his voice calm and reassuring. "Merry Christmas," he repeats, looking down at me as I try to move my arms. My body seems like a lifeless glob of spongy rubber. My feet are no longer crossed. I am unable to talk coherently through my blubbering saliva. Warm tears wash my eyes.

"You just lie still, Sweetie. You've had open-heart surgery — again. Jim and I will dry your tears, and a few of our own, then we'll rearrange every one of your pillows. I'm sure glad you're finally awake." Dave's voice reflects my excitement, too. "This is Christmas Eve morning! It is now 7:11 a.m. on a pretty sunshiny Sunday morning."

"Oh shit!" was not meant to be my Christmas salutation to the two Green Men who had watched over me on the night shift for the seven long nights of my coma. These first angry garbled words I know I had said aloud embarrassed me. This obscenity is my pet expression of turmoil when my back is against the wall.

My Christmas shopping is not finished. The special cuts of beef I had ordered for my grandson and his wife as their chosen holiday gifts have not been picked up. This is December 24th. What am I to do?

My apology is countered with Green Men laughter and, "Sure. Sure."

Tears veiling blue, blue eyes of happiness later assure me that Santa will return with many gifts, as I am deluged with hugs and kisses.

My real bouquet of pretty balloons becomes true. Then a mixed media of questions and answers with my surgeons and cardiologist, about my lost days and nights, unnerve me.

"Was I dying during my coma? True? I didn't hear the sound of angels' wings or the rattle of the devil's pitchfork, but...fellows...I did see and feel the comfort of a calming beacon from a very pleasant immense silky, white light hovering about me...at times. I...I have a few questions about that light. Did all go well?"

"Finally, Nadine," my cardiologist assures me. "But, for a few frantic moments during your touch-and-go surgery we thought...at times...we'd lost all life from your body. Enjoy those pretty red balloons, Kid, and welcome back home."

The doctors' eyes hold questions that have no answers.

JANELLE MERAZ HOOPER

# This Far From Homeless

There it was — the chalk. Macky had to have it before he went home. He couldn't take his eyes off its slender form as it rested on the powdery tray below the blackboard about six feet away from the front door to the office.

Macky paced back and forth nervously on the sidewalk outside. He had to be careful not to alert the secretary that he was watching the chalk. Watching her. He could have scrounged enough money to buy a piece of chalk, but where? Stores in downtown Seattle didn't sell piddley stuff like chalk.

It was getting late; he had to make his move soon. Not only would the office be closing, but a storm was on the way. There was no door and no lock to his home on the street; if he didn't get back soon, someone else might move in. His friend, Leo, always tried to save him a spot, but he was a small man, and no match against the bigger homeless men who slept underneath the freeway overpass. There was enough space under the bridge to keep eight men dry on a cold, rainy night. No more. It was first come, first serve — unless a man bigger than you wanted your spot. Whenever that happened, the best thing to do was just roll up your bedroll and skidaddle. No spot was worth dying over.

If Macky was late, he'd be forced to spend the night in the shelter. He would be off the street and the food was hot, but it was a dangerous place to be late at night. Robberies and beatings were common once the supervisors lowered the lights and went downstairs. Leo had been rolled there last year.

Macky turned his attention back to the office. The secretary was getting up and going to the back room, probably to get her coat.

Macky took a nervous breath and rushed through the door. Ignoring the woman's purse, he grabbed the piece of white chalk and ran back outside. As he did, he heard her call out, "Who's there? Is anybody there?" He grabbed his grocery cart and was halfway down the block before he dared to slow down. His knees were weak and his heart pounded. Sweat from his brow mixed with the first drops of rain.

Who knew what might happen if he got caught stealing? The new mayor was cracking down on street people. If he were jailed, his spot under the overpass would be gone for sure by the time he got out. None of the street people knew what to expect right now. Lately, they knew they could be arrested merely for jaywalking.

The craziness wouldn't last forever. Macky knew that in a few weeks the mayor would tire of timing the traffic lights, intimidating the jaywalkers, and hassling the street people. Then things would go back to normal. Every new mayor was the same.

No one noticed a ragged Macky racing a cart with every worldly possession he had in the direction of the industrial area. Everyone was scrambling, head down, trying to get out of the weather before the storm hit, some of them gulping coffee to celebrate the end of another work day. As he raced by the office workers, the fragrant smell of Starbuck's coffee invaded his nose. Longingly he glanced in the coffee shop window. He had enough money to buy a small cup of coffee, but he didn't have enough time to stand in line. Luckily, he didn't have to. A sympathetic young barista, with every raised part of his young face pierced with tarnished silver rings, rushed out and — keeping pace with Macky — gave him a 12-ouncer.

"Have a nice night, Macky."

Macky nodded and mumbled a thank you. He'd stop by in the morning and sweep the sidewalk in front of the shop. He'd clean the outside tables too. The sparrows that slept up in the trees at night dirtied the outside seating area. Macky had been helping out at the coffee shop for a couple of years. It made him feel good to help, and it was a way to pay for the free coffees that came his way. It didn't matter to him that the coffees were leftovers that customers had decided — for whatever reason — they didn't want.

Macky patted the lid of the steaming coffee. Maybe it would bring him luck tonight. He didn't take a sip right away. He'd save it until he got home so he could share it with Leo and Hazel, his neighbors.

The closer Macky got to his home, the faster he picked up his pace. The grimy raincoat that was almost in shreds sailed outward behind him, exposing to the rain his Visit Las Vegas sweatshirt and World War II vintage green wool pants. His shoes were separating from the soles and his sockless feet were crusted with dirt that softened when he ran through a mud puddle. Even his dark hair, thick with the grease of neglect, raised slightly as air rushed underneath it, like the wings of a too-heavy airplane trying to lift off a runway. His eyes strained ahead to see if Leo was at the underpass, but his concrete home was still too far away. Passing trucks, pedestrians, and buildings obstructed his view.

Finally, he caught sight of Leo rushing from the other direction. He was late too. Macky's heart sank; they were doomed to a shelter for the night. They were both out of breath when they arrived at the underpass. Amazed, they found it almost deserted. Only Hazel squatted in her usual spot. She wasn't feeling well so she hadn't gone downtown to panhandle.

Leo told the two he was a victim of a prank while he slept on a bench in Pioneer Square. The badge the young pranksters had pinned on his jacket lapel pictured a woman with boobs that blinked. He hadn't taken it off, and Macky sensed that for some reason he was afraid to.

"Where is everybody?" Macky asked the shivering woman.

"They all left. The storm drain is plugged up. The cars are throwing water all over the sidewalk."

"We've got to fix it." Macky shouted. "Quick, before it gets dark." Macky dove into the gutter and fished around with his hands, pulling out clumps of garbage, grass, and discarded paper. All the time he worked, he was watchful of passing cars.

Leo went to work soaking up the wet cement with wads of newspapers. The water would only be a problem until the commuter traffic was over. After that, the road saw little traffic.

Macky reached in his pocket and tossed the chalk to Hazel, who silently went to work drawing their living rooms. Even though no one else was there and she could have used all the space she wanted, Hazel drew the same size rectangle for each person. Six feet long, three feet wide. Each shape joined the next for safety, even though the rules of the street said no other homeless person would infringe on their territory. The same rules were not honored by people who didn't live on the street; regularly, strangers thoughtlessly walked through the trio's living rooms. That wouldn't be a problem tonight; the weather would discourage foot traffic.

Meanwhile, Macky was joined by Leo who used an old discarded pool cue he had in his cart to probe the drain and try to loosen the blockage. Finally, the two heard a swoosh of water as the drain cleared and the water ran freely down the gutter and away through the drain.

The coffee was still untouched, although they could all smell it. It would wait until they had their homes set up. Macky meticulously lined up all of his possessions in a straight line on the inside front edge of his living room walled in chalk. There was a tin can with three new cigarettes and a little chipped dish. He added a cracked candleholder with the candle still in it that he'd found behind a restaurant. Leo lined up his newspaper that they'd all share before he put it underneath his bedroll to insulate himself against the cold, with some cigar stubs, and a tiny tablet and pencil stub. Hazel set out a little framed photo of her daughter at her college graduation. It was protected by a resealable bag she had fished out of a garbage can.

Meanwhile, the workers in their shiny commuter cars rushed by the squatters, pausing only when the traffic slowed to stare curiously at the chalk outlines and the little treasures displayed in a neat line in front of each rectangle. The three and their living rooms would be forgotten by the time the cars went through the Spring Street intersection.

Up ahead, Macky could see the flashing yellow lights of a police motorcycle. The Grannies were coming, driving their old beat up yellow import with the hatch back. They stopped at all of the underpasses in the area two or three times a week, bringing hot sandwiches and coffee to their fellow humans. The food was purchased with their meager pension checks, assembled with love, and dispensed with grace. The first time one of the women handed a shivering Macky a sandwich, he asked her, "Why are you doing this?" The woman answered, "Because I know that all of us are just *this* far from homeless." As she talked, she held up her thumb and index finger — almost touching.

Then, with a smile and a wave, she was gone. She and the rest of the Grannies didn't make them uncomfortable by insisting on praying with them. The women didn't try to change their lifestyle. They didn't try to make them ashamed of their circumstances. The Grannies' no-strings-attached gifts of food and drink were the only outside contact most of the street people had.

Macky split the coffee from the barista three ways so they could drink it with their sandwiches. It was still warm, thanks to their feverish activity. The coffee from the Grannies would be saved until breakfast. Even though it would be cold by then, they'd be glad to have it.

The winds were just beginning to pick up as they took their first sips. The group was quiet; no one would talk about their day. Hazel would not reveal the ever-widening ulcer on a varicose vein on her left leg — right above her happy-face tattoo — that Macky had spotted days ago. Macky would not mention to Leo that Leo's Microsoft stock had split today — he knew his friend wouldn't be interested. Macky only knew about it because Leo had sold some of his stock when he'd needed money last year after he was hit by a truck that jumped the curb. Macky, too, had his secrets: he would not mention his terrifying chalk experience or the businessman who had tried to spit on him as he crossed an intersection.

Most of all, they would not talk about the choices they'd made in their lives that brought them to huddle night after night under a cold wet overpass.

The commuter traffic slowed. As it darkened, the candle in Macky's living room radiated a soft glow that bounced off the wet pavement and threw shadows on the back wall of the overpass. They were home for the night. It was cold and wet, but they were safe for another day. Tomorrow, they'd get up and start all over again.

JAMES FRANCIS SMITH

# Sadie and Abigail

Sadie, who had never been a good driver, enjoyed the bus ride across the Narrows Bridge almost as much as she gloated over downtown Tacoma's new construction. *Has it really been eighteen years since I've ventured downtown?*

The Glass Museum, elegant condos along the waterfront, and the many new high-rise office buildings amazed her. Like a tourist, she gazed through the tinted-glass window of the light-rail car that carried her along Pacific Avenue. Sadie alighted in front of the one building that hadn't changed. The building directory indicated that her husband's former employer, the law firm of Wilson, Taft and Hoover (WT&H) had grown phenomenally, and currently occupied four floors. The elevator rose swiftly past the WT&H domain to the twenty-third floor penthouse. Sadie gasped when she emerged into a living-room atmosphere instead of the stark hallway she had anticipated.

"Good morning, you must be Sadie Baker. I'm Luanne, Ms. Wentworth's receptionist," said the slim blonde, who dressed as if she stepped out of Vogue magazine. "Please make yourself comfortable. Abigail is on the phone, but she will be with you shortly. May I serve you some tea or coffee?"

Observing that Luanne offered tea before coffee, a feminist trait, Sadie accepted the tea. Had she known that the receptionist's responsibilities included sizing up new clients, Sadie would have agreed with her observation: quality clothes but a bit out of fashion, middle-aged and well-to-do.

"May I validate your parking receipt while you're waiting?"

"That won't be necessary," Sadie answered while seating herself in one of the comfortable mauve-colored upholstered lounge chairs. She looked around and mentally complimented the decorator.

Sipping hot tea while enjoying a ladyfinger, she thought about how to deal with Abigail Wentworth, a highly respected legal barracuda. Sadie's lady friends lavished praise on the successful divorce attorney, particularly her courtroom victories.

While Sadie bided her time in the reception area, Abigail opened the folder that an assistant had just handed her. She always waited until the buzzer signaled a client's arrival before reviewing the information supplied by her research department. Abigail smiled when she encountered Dennis Baker's name and wondered why anyone would have stayed married to that lecher for so many years. Perhaps today she would find the answer.

Making pencil notations, she recalled her one and only encounter with Dennis. It had occurred after the two had tangled in court and he offered to buy her a congratulatory drink. Aware of his reputation but ignoring her instincts, she accepted his offer. One drink became several before Dennis made his move. Instead of rejecting his advances outright, Abigail hesitated long enough to consider what it would feel like to have sex with Tacoma's best-known adulterer. Common sense finally overruled curiosity and she turned him down. Only later did it occur to her that his offer had insulted both her professionalism and her female pride.

Noting that he resided on the far side of the Narrows Bridge, she assumed that Dennis led two lives, a respectable family man in Gig Harbor and a Casanova in Tacoma. If that's so, he probably has an apartment on this side of the bridge, which means he hid assets from his spouse. Smiling, she made a note to check into that aspect.

A surprise awaited Sadie when the double oak doors opened and a pleasant looking, well-groomed businesswoman emerged with her hands outstretched in greeting. "Hello, Sadie. Don't look so shocked; I save my wrath for the courtroom — I'm delighted that we have finally met. I've heard about your charitable works, and I commend you for taking an interest in our community's homeless. Please come into my office." She directed Sadie to one of a pair of comfortable chairs separated by an oval coffee table. The spacious room resembled anything but an office. The decorator had continued the same mauve color throughout the chairs and drapes. There were several inlaid oak bookshelves; however, Sadie noted there was neither a desk nor a telephone.

"I notice you looking around and I know you are wondering how

I accomplish any work. The usual office utensils are cleverly hidden behind that revolving fake fireplace. I originally contracted the decorator for my home on Gravelly Lake. He did such splendid work that I engaged him for my two offices. His taste and creativity enable my clients to relax, and, believe me, many of them desperately need relaxation. Before we begin the formal part of our meeting, I'm curious about how you developed such instinctive observation skills."

"I came into this world as a sharecropper's daughter," Sadie answered. "My father taught me to study and copy the style and mannerisms of folks who were better off. You might say that I became an actress at a very young age."

"I'm impressed. You seem to be well informed; therefore, you must know that maintaining two offices is bloody expensive. Once a divorce is finalized, regardless of the outcome, few people desire to meet their obligations. Therefore, I have made it a rule to insist on a twenty-five percent deposit up front. Your divorce from a practicing attorney will take a significant outlay of time and energy; consequently, I require a twenty-five thousand dollar check before we continue."

Sadie took a checkbook from her purse and filled in the required amount. Abigail studied the out-of-state financial instrument for a few moments before slipping it into the folder on the coffee table. The delay didn't go unnoticed by Sadie who asked, "You are supposed to keep our conversations secret, aren't you?"

"Yes, I am. That's the essence of attorney-client privilege," she replied just a bit curious about the secrets this lady knew about Dennis. "Tell me why, after all this time, you want a divorce? Are you having marital problems?"

"Dennis and I *hate* each other and always have," Sadie answered without any show of emotion.

The attorney's widened eyes indicated that Sadie's use of such a strong verb unsettled her. Abigail hesitated before asking, "Why divorce now after all these years?"

"It's a long story that needs to be told from the beginning to make any sense."

"I have made an hour and a half available," Abigail said. "Besides, I charge by the hour." The two ladies snickered over the oft-told lawyer's joke.

"Sam, my first husband suffered a massive heart attack and died while I drove him to the hospital," Sadie continued.

"Why didn't you call an ambulance or tell the police about Sam's condition?"

"Perhaps I wanted him dead. At least, that's what Dennis thinks."

"Why would he think that?"

"Because that's what I want him to think. That, and the purchase of a small pistol, enabled me to keep him at a distance for almost the entire length of our marriage."

"Go on."

"He needed a wife to disguise his philandering from his Gig Harbor clients and I desperately needed a 'sugar daddy' to pay off my debts. We entered into a temporary marital arrangement."

"Tell me about Dennis."

"He lost his mother when he turned six-years old, and was raised by his father, who blamed their dismal life on the mother's desertion. This had a sadistic impact on his outlook on women. I took a job with him when he opened his own law practice. About the same time, he nearly lost his best client. The client demanded that Dennis become a respectable married man or he would take his business elsewhere. Desperate because of my enormous financial burden, I made a pact with the devil. Dennis agreed to pay off my debts if I pretended to be his faithful wife for a period of three years. I consented when he accepted my terms that we would never engage in sexual relations."

"Three years have turned into eighteen. How come?"

"A few months after the start of our mock marriage, he received a large retainer and bought a bottle of champagne to celebrate. I got drunk and pregnant. I stayed with Dennis as his token wife to insure that my daughter would never be as desperate as I had once been."

"Did you achieve financial independence or is that the goal of the divorce?"

"Dennis has absolutely no taste — neither in food nor clothing. I pretended to purchase clothes at Nordstrom and other exclusive establishments. The clothes actually came from the Salvation Army. I sewed on Nordstrom labels, poured cheap wine into expensive bottles and squirreled away money any way that I could."

"That explains the out-of-state bank account."

"In addition to a bank account, I have a sizeable stock account with a Chicago broker. My daughter will never want for anything," Sadie said defiantly.

"Why are you seeking a divorce *now*?"

"My daughter is about to graduate from Annie Wright Academy. She plans to attend Bryn Mawr College outside Philadelphia. I intend to relocate and live near her."

"You believe that Dennis would attempt to stop you?"

"Dennis would do anything within his power to keep me as his token wife, particularly now."

"Why particularly now?"

"There is something else that you should know about our marital relations. I had sex with Dennis one time only. Since then he has sought his sexual gratification elsewhere, sometimes with prostitutes, employees and even live-in maids."

"You still haven't answered my question!"

"I'm getting to your question. Dennis changed from picking up local prostitutes along South Tacoma Way to picking up prostitutes along Pacific Avenue near SeaTac airport. For some time, I suspected that he might be the Green River Killer."

"You suspected Dennis of being the Green River killer?" a stunned Abigail repeated.

"Yes! Dennis had all the characteristics. He possessed an unnatural need to control women, and he frequented the area where the Green River killer selected his victims. What greater control could Dennis attain than killing his conquest after he had sexually satisfied himself?"

A shaken Abigail asked her next question. "How do you know all this?"

"I hired a detective to follow him," Sadie answered coolly. "Unfortunately, the police accused someone else of the killings."

"Did you just find this out? Is this why you're seeking a divorce?"

"No, there is one more thing that you should know. Dennis has AIDS."

"He has AIDS?" an even more shaken Abigail asked.

"Yes! I administer medicine to him every day, without which he would die. Now that you know all this, what are my chances for getting a divorce?"

"Give me a few minutes to think. Please have some more tea."

Abigail selected several documents from the built-in bookcases and began to make notes on a yellow legal pad. Meanwhile, Sadie watched out the window as an ocean-bound freighter sailed from the Port of Tacoma. The ship had already reached the deep-water channel alongside Vashon Island before Abigail returned to the conference area.

"First I would like to discuss the financial implications," the lawyer said. "Washington is a community property state, which means the entire income earned during your marriage belongs equally to both of you. One-half of the balance in your out-of-state accounts legally belongs to Dennis. Any divorce lawyer worth their salt will discover your secret funds in a search for hidden assets. Just as I will discover any of Dennis' hidden assets.

"This case will surely go to trial before a male judge because most divorce case judges are male. Male judges instinctively side with the male participant. Inevitably, the judge will compensate for Dennis' medical condition by awarding him an amount significantly greater than his legal share of the combined assets.

"I recommend that you pursue a divorce only if you and your daughter can survive on the remaining twenty-five percent, minus my fee."

Sadie left after agreeing to reconsider her options. Before boarding the light-rail train to return to the bus terminal, she made a decision. "I'll just have to keep watering down his medicine."

## CHARLOTTE RICHARDS

# Final Retribution

Charlie Harper woke up suddenly from a frightful nightmare. In his dream he was on fire. He could still see the flames licking up around him, devouring him, roasting his flesh like a freshly slaughtered pig on a spit. The vision was so vivid he felt like vomiting from the oily, burning smell which still lingered in his nostrils.

Thank God he was awake. But why was he still breathing that smoky stench, that whiff of burning ash? He suppressed an involuntary sneeze.

*I have to get up and see what's going on,* he thought. *Maybe the fire's still burning from that big log I put in the fireplace last night.* But when he tried to get out of bed he bumped against the wall. "Must have had too much to drink before I hit the sack," he muttered. Trying to roll out on the other side, he found he was still hemmed in by a solid wall. When he tried to stand up, he banged his head on an unyielding barrier directly above him.

His heart began pounding like a trip hammer. *Oh, God, maybe I wasn't home last night after all. Maybe I was hijacked drunk in a bar while I was with some bimbo and now I'm on my way to China.* He listened for the chugging of diesel engines or the churning of water. Nothing. Absolute silence. An even more insidious thought began to steal into his mind. *I've been buried alive! I must have gone into a coma and everybody thought I was dead. But I'm alive! I'm still alive!*

Then he heard the sound of a voice. Marie! She must have come to the graveyard to mourn his untimely death. She'd get him out. She wouldn't let him die. In a panic he began to scream, "Marie! I'm not dead! Let me out!" In dismay he realized that he was unable to utter a single sound.

A ghastly thought grabbed him by the throat and choked off his breath. Maybe it was Marie who had made sure he was buried alive. Come to think of it, that last drink she had fixed him…when was it?…he couldn't remember…had tasted a little bitter. She must have put something in it that knocked him unconscious and paralyzed his vocal cords.

He listened with rising apprehension to her crooning voice.

"Now, my sweetums, there's just you and me. My darling little Maxie will never have to worry about that awful, mean man hurting a precious hair on your head again. And he'll never be able to cheat on me again, either. I've taken care of that forever." He heard soft panting sounds as she laughed wickedly.

Good God! The woman was insane! She had buried him alive because he kicked her nasty little floor mop of a dog. What was he supposed to do when the creature insisted on lifting his leg on Charlie's shoe every time he walked in the door? As for cheating, there were only Tammy and Christy. Oh, yes, and Brandy, too; he almost forgot about her. But they were just minor flings. Nothing to commit murder over.

He could hear Max growling softly as Marie came closer to Charlie's grave. Had Marie come to gloat, or was she planning to dig Charlie up, thinking that she had finally taught him a lesson? Trying to gulp in as much musty air as he could, he made a fervent promise to whatever Powers That Be that if he were freed from his prison, he would never raise a foot to Max or chase blonde bimbos again.

Suddenly Charlie could feel motion. What was happening? Then he could hear squeaking, as if Marie had sat down in a chair. How could that be? Maybe she had buried him in the backyard and was planning to guard the site until he died a tortuous death from suffocation.

Next he heard a sound like a lid lifting and his prison was flooded with light. Oh, thank God, Marie had decided to free him. In his joy he pledged to lead a better life in the future, be more romantic to Marie, and….

But before he could finish his thought, he began to experience a weird and unsettling feeling of disorientation. It was as if all the minute particles of his body were sifting like powdery ashes through Marie's fingers. He must be hallucinating from the terror of being buried alive. Then his mind did a quick double take. Ashes! Marie hadn't buried him. She had cremated him! That's why he had had the nightmare of being set on fire. It wasn't a nightmare! It was real!

Charlie thought desperately, *But if I'm dead and my body is cremated, why am I still able to hear and feel?* He had always sneered at the religious belief that the souls of the wicked are sent to hell to burn in everlasting fire. "How can a soul without a body feel fire?" he had always maintained with scorn.

Since he was able to ponder all of these things in his present state of physical nonbeing, it must be true that souls retain consciousness after death and that they can still feel mental and physical pain. He had already passed through fire, so he wondered if being imprisoned in a funeral urn was to be his eternal hell or if a final, and more terrible, retribution was still to come.

The chime of the doorbell interrupted his morbid thoughts. He felt himself being jostled and set down. Marie said to the dog, "I have to see who's at the door, sweetie. But now that I've shown you Charlie's ashes, you know he's really dead and won't ever come back to hurt you."

After Marie left the room he could hear Max put his paws up on the end table and sniff the urn holding Charlie's ashes. "Go away, Max!" he silently willed. Then he heard a soft growl, followed by an eerie sensation of disintegration as the urn crashed to the floor and spilled Charlie's remains all over the living room rug. He was aware of the dog standing over him triumphantly and knew instantly what was about to happen. "No, Max, no!" he wailed in a soundless voice as Max lifted his leg and Charlie began dissolving and seeping slowly into the living room carpet.

MICHAEL ROBBINS

# Doppelganger Effect

If it hadn't been for the rage he might have seen this coming. God, he couldn't believe he did that. He couldn't blame her for what she did. Funny, though, that gunshot to the head didn't hurt now.

Ambulance lights strobed red and white. Why wouldn't they give him another blanket? It was like Antarctica outside. He hadn't the strength to turn his head, or much else. Voices, probably paramedics, shouting…what? They drifted in from so far away. Barely felt the straps locking him to the gurney.

How could he have done this? His own baby. What if they hauled Maggie off to jail? She'd been in foster care. They swore before they even got married that they'd never abuse their child the way they had been abused. Well, that one sure went out the window, didn't it?

Some fat cow in a dowdy sweater had walked into their apartment a few minutes earlier. Then she walked out, stone-faced, carrying their squalling infant Chelsea in her arms while Maggie screamed, begged, pleaded with the officer restraining her on the doorstep.

At least the cop had some sympathy. "Don't you think you're going overboard?" he said to Stone-face. "He only put his hand over the kid's mouth."

*Only…?* Wasn't that bad enough? Paddles floated over his chest as darkness shuttered his eyes. If he could go back he'd damn well have a few words with himself. Voltage crackled into his heart, and it actually jumped, for a couple beats anyhow.

A part of him slid Jell-O-like from his shell, full of purpose.

The baby cried and cried as desperate as the night they'd brought her home two weeks before. Her wails homed in on the back of his skull and bored into the bone. Theirs was a typical one-bedroom apartment, basically a hole in the wail. The hand-me-down couch took up half the living area. The stereo cabinet and big-screen TV took up the other corner, beside the books Maggie left in every bare spot. So there wasn't far for the shrieks to travel.

He'd left Chelsea in the car seat after driving her around town for a half-hour. He didn't want to risk waking her by transferring her to her crib. Two minutes earlier she'd still been fast asleep. He'd just pulled the covers up over himself when she went off again.

Why couldn't she shut up...shut up...shut up! He jammed his hand over her tiny mouth trying to stifle her screams, screaming himself as Maggie shrieked from the bedroom, "Stop it! Stop it! She's only a baby!"

How could she criticize him about this? She'd been the one puking her guts out for nine months, getting him out of bed at all hours of the night to go to the hospital. She must've been in and out of emergency seven times for dehydration alone. She almost died having this baby! It was supposed to be over now!

Jesus H. Christ, the baby wouldn't eat, she wouldn't sleep. All she did was cry, cry, CRY! He hadn't had a solid night's sleep in weeks. What did it take to satisfy this brat?

A sudden force shoved him to the wall. Hands shook him like he was a baby himself. His hands...worse, his face! "What the hell's the matter with you!" he shouted. "She's just a baby! Can't you see she's colicky?"

He shoved...what, himself?...away, and slumped to the floor. "Get away from me, I can't handle it anymore!" he said. "Nothing I do does any good! I don't know what to do..."

"Maybe you should get away from her. You're scaring the shit out of her. Babies sense those things."

His hands trembled, partly from rage but also from a dawning horror. The kid really was terrified of him. Maybe that was the biggest problem. But then he stared at his other self. "Hey, how did you get here?"

"It doesn't matter. No one's called Child Protection...nobody knows. You still have a chance to undo this."

"For Chrissakes, I attacked my own daughter! How can I...?"

"First, get on your knees and apologize to your daughter. Then get some help for that shitty temper of yours. Do you hear me, you fucking idiot? Get-some-help!"

A swift backhand broadsided him in the head for good measure. He tumbled into the back of the couch as his other self loomed over him. He stared into this other's livid, insane eyes…his own eyes.

He craned his neck so he could view Chelsea in her car seat, upside-down. What was he doing? God knows they didn't hate Chelsea. They'd waited two years to have a baby girl, gone through too much to lose her.

His other self stepped back as the bedroom door hinges creaked. Maggie walked through on trembling legs, clutching their handgun. She must have taken it from the shoebox in the closet. But it was pointed at his reflection, not him.

"Don't you dare hurt my baby," she said. "Eric, for God's sake, see about Chelsea."

He crawled past himself around their ratty couch and threw his arms over the car seat. Not in anger this time, but as a shield. Chelsea gazed up at him with bright, curious eyes. Her eyes flickered, and for that moment he seemed to share a crazy thought with his reflection. The baby was all right…would be all right now.

Maggie hadn't fired, but her attention strayed as his body shuddered. His ribs ached with sobs. He had to keep his hands around the seat; he couldn't stand to look at them. His stomach churned as he realized how close he'd come to being an abuser like his own parents.

Maggie slowly set the pistol on the floor beside him. "We gotta get help," she said. Somehow, coming from her it didn't sound so awful. He nodded.

Maybe that's all the other needed. His word had always meant something to him; usually it was all he had to give. When he…or they…said he would do it, it was done. The other saluted and grinned. "See ya."

They of course never noticed his passing, because for all intents and purposes he had never even been there.

PATRICIA LAWTON

# Smiling Faces; Deadly Places

I can still hear the click of her high heels on the cement sidewalk. It is 1953, eight years after the war. My father is stationed in Kaiserslaughtern, Germany. The housing project and base are called Volgaweh. I can see castle ruins on the rise above us. My friends and I play in bomb craters disguised by the trees.

My mother has let me stay late in the movie theater with my friend Carol. She is ten and I am eight. We run over the wooden arch bridge which spans the two-lane highway. We like to pretend there are trolls under it. Ahead of us is a curved sidewalk, to the left apartments four stories high, to the right a dark wooded area. The sidewalk goes up the middle with about one hundred feet on each side. Up ahead a baseball field looms on the apartment side. A couple of blocks past the woods is our apartment building. A woman walks ahead of us by herself. We hurry around and pass her, then I look over my shoulder.

"Gutentag," she says as she nods with a smile.

We giggle and go on. We slow our pace then. There is a silence. The high heels are not clicking anymore on the sidewalk. Has she turned to walk through the field?

Screams erupt from the woods. They stop. Then erupt again. My friend and I look at each other. No one comes out of the apartments. I want to run back, but I am afraid. The woods seem much closer. We run home. I will tell my parents; she will tell hers.

Safe inside, I tell my mother, but she won't listen. I threaten to go outside to a neighbor. We don't have a phone. There are no 911 numbers. She tells me I will be in big trouble. The door to the staircase may as well be bolted with huge locks. I fear opening it. Maybe Carol's parents will listen.

Later in the week, my mother is reading *Stars and Stripes*. She looks at me. A woman has been found in the woods by the bridge. Her throat has been slashed. A Polish man has done it. She is a young German girl who works and lives in the apartments — each apartment had a maid's room. The Polish man hates Germans.

My mother and I live forty years more as best friends. That incident is never discussed.

Ten years from that date, 1963. I am traipsing up to Mt. Rainier with my first true love. I am eighteen. I have followed him around cliffs on the Michael River. It has been dry going up, with easy handholds. A storm strikes without warning. The water rages below us. Now I am scared nearly to death. The wet rocks and handholds are slippery. He says I can do it. I cannot swim, but I am young and in love. I protest, but I follow and make it without mishap. On we go up to the mountain. Once again the weather returned to one of those perfect days — balmy, beautiful, sweet smelling.

I enjoy the drive up. We come to the Nisqually Glacier. It is the source of the Nisqually River. A bridge crosses the headwaters. We pull into the parking area under the bridge. He asks me if I want to walk to the glacier. It sounds like fun. I want to get as near to the face of the glacier as I can. It's a long walk; we go around a huge boulder — big as a house. It is still there. We work our way past it. Up ahead is a waterfall we can walk around or under. I am enchanted when I walk under the falling cascade. I go under the falls again, returning after we go as far up as we can. As we descend, three couples are approaching on the path. They are enjoying the day also. I smile; they smile back. We are sharing a perfect day. I excitedly tell them that they can walk under the waterfall. We continue down the trail, past the huge rock.

Do I hear something? I look back. Nothing — the boulder blocks my view.

The road down the mountain is wonderful. A light rain makes a rainbow bridging the open valley below — a beautiful sign of things to come. The next day we read in the newspaper that within minutes of the time we were at the falls, it collapsed, killing three people. We look at each other in the selfishness of youth. It could have been us.

JODI SULLIVAN

# The Devil May Care

C laws tore at Valerie's flesh while low guttural sounds ema-
nated from the creature above her. In the red cast darkness
she could just make out his face.

"Oh my God," she screamed.

Then the burn began, a warm bead in her gut growing until it
felt like molten rock.

Ten months later...at The Perkins Sanatorium:

> Patient File
>
> Name: *Valerie DeVilbride*
> Sex: *Female*
> Condition: *Postpartum Trauma. Patient arrived at
> Perkins in a state of clinical hysteria following
> childbirth. Patient is delusional regarding a male
> personage in her room.*
> *Ms. DeVilbride's infant will be placed for adoption,
> as patient continues to display violent intentions
> toward the child, convinced that he is a menace to
> the world.*
> Prognosis: *Irreversible mental incapacitation.
> Patient is not expected to recover.*

I n a locked room Valerie thought back to the first time Luc had
come to her. She had been terrified that night when her father
turned off the light, slammed the door, and left her to "learn to deal
with it" — *it* being the monsters that had lived in her bedroom since
her earliest memory. She became aware of their presence whenever
her parents tucked her in and turned off the light. She always called

43

her dad back to check the closet and under the bed. Monsters are afraid of fathers. By age twelve that had been her bedtime ritual for nearly nine years.

On that particular night her father and mother had been arguing. "What the hell is the matter with her?" Father yelled. "She's twelve years old, and I still have to chase monsters out of her room. You baby her too much and I'm getting sick of it!" He jumped up, spilling his drink. Leaving the whiskey dripping onto the carpet and taking the stairs two at a time, he went up to her room.

"I'm sorry, Val, but your mom and I are separating. I'm moving out." His voice hardened. "Your monsters are not real and you need to learn to deal with it!"

When he left the room, she lay in the dark, terrified, afraid to move. She could feel the creatures near her. They would pounce if she moved, so she continued to lie in the dark, barely breathing. Long slow breaths. Quiet breaths. Her heart pounded. Surely they could hear it. "Don't move, don't move!" she thought.

"Hi."

"What?" she thought, too terrified to answer.

"Hello?" he said. "It's okay now. You can talk to me."
Slowly Val opened her eyes, half expecting to see a drooling monster waiting to take a bite of her. What she saw first was a self-assured, somewhat cocky grin attached to a very cute boy. He sat in the chair at the end of her bed. His sneaker-clad feet were on top of her coverlet, just next to hers.

"I'm Luc, like Luke, spelled L-U-C. I came to chase your monsters away. Take a look around: You'll notice that I'm pretty good at it." He gestured around the room. There was a warm glow to the room and no monsters.

Val sighed and started to breathe normally. "Thank you, Luc."

"No problem, little one. I'll come back tomorrow night if you'd like."

"Yes. Please."

"Okay, but I can only come after you are asleep."

"Why?" she asked, suddenly afraid again.

"Because it's my way, but I'll take care of the monsters before you go to sleep. You can count on me."

"Will you wake me when you come?"

"I won't need to. You'll know I'm here."

Valerie looked thoughtful. "Am I asleep now?"

"Yes."

44

When Valerie woke the sun was shining and she felt good. The dream had been a good one and that Luc kid had been so nice. He seemed real, as dreams often do. Too bad he wasn't. She could use a friend like him.

When she went downstairs she found her mother sitting at the kitchen table, her eyes red and puffy.

"Honey," her mother began, "your daddy has gone. He'll be staying at Uncle Jack's until he can find a house of his own. You may see him on weekends."

"But Mom, can he tuck me in at night?" Tears filled her own eyes.

"No, Baby, but I will," her mother offered.

"Thanks, Mom," Valerie said, knowing full well that the monsters would get her now. They only listened to her dad.

Valerie was more shy and withdrawn than usual that day. She stuttered and stammered her way through an oral report at school. The other kids laughed. They teased her. The more they tormented, the more withdrawn she became.

The place where Val found her happiness was with Luc. True to his word, he had returned the night following his appearance in her dream. Val's mother tucked her snuggly into bed and performed the ritual search for monsters. Val lay terrified despite her mother's efforts, knowing that sharp teeth and claws would soon reach her flesh. She held her breath, then out of sheer necessity, let it out silently. Ready to scream at the first tearing of skin and muscle from her bones, she wondered how it would feel when they finally got her — those creatures that had plagued her for so long.

"You can breathe now, you know," Luc said.

Startled, Valerie nearly let out a scream. Instead it came out as a yelp. She whispered, "Luc, is that you?"

"You expecting someone else in the middle of the night?"

"No...no, I just..."

"I know," he grinned, " I'm just too good to be true!"

She sat up and took a good look at him. She too smiled. God, he is cute, she thought.

"I am here for the long haul, you know. The monsters are gone. They won't be back as long as I'm here. So, let's see a smile for ol' Luc." When he tilted her chin their eyes met. In that split second she knew she could trust him, knew that he cared. She was startled at his touch and at the warmth of his skin.

As if reading her thoughts, Luc said simply, "I am real Valerie. I just live in the night."

"Well, you're real to me right now," she stated boldly. "Let's do something fun!" Valerie felt good. She felt strong and confident. Luc was good for her.

He took her to a beautiful dark place where the grass was soft, the breeze warm. She saw the same red glow that had been in her room the first time Luc had been there. They ran and played, laughed and joked. Sometimes they lay in the grass watching the night sky, talking about the future.

"When I was little, I wanted to be a princess," Val confided.

"I am the prince of the nighttime!" he exclaimed. "You shall be my princess!" He smiled at her, then leaned over and kissed her cheek. His lips were soft, his gray eyes gentle. A lock of blond hair fell across his forehead and Valerie reached up to brush it back. He caught her hand, pressed it to his chest where his heart beat wildly, then he kissed her full on the mouth.

Valerie blossomed in her teens. She had learned to ignore her classmates, but the boys began to notice her. When on occasion one of them would ask her out, she would smile and say, "Sorry, there is someone else." They thought it strange that she had never been seen with a boy, nor did she attend school activities or dances. In time her peers came to realize that Valerie was a loner.

Her mother worried because Val's free time was spent in her room listening to music and napping. She wondered how a girl could sleep as much as Valerie did and yet wake unrested. When she asked about it, Valerie simply stated that, "Not all sleep is restful." Her mother accepted her answer and moved on with her own concerns. After Valerie graduated, her mother began making plans to remarry.

Val made her own plans to move out. She rented a small apart-ment, furnished it with a good quality bed, a small table, a few dishes and a computer on which she did data processing to support herself. Her nights  were spent with Luc. She was nineteen then, and very much in love with the dream man. They had grown up together, he into a hand-some man, muscled and fit, she into a woman whose wispy child-hood curls had thickened to a glorious crown of ebony. Her brown eyes framed in long lashes were set above a well-shaped nose and full soft lips.

One night as they romped in the gardens of his night land, Val confided to Luc that she wished she could spend eternity with him.

He laughed. "Be careful what you wish for. It could come true!"

Then he ran off and she followed. Luc pretended to trip and fall near some strange iris-like flowers. He snapped one off at the stem and held it out to her. She had to sit down next to him to reach it.

"You're an angel," she said.

"That's me, a fallen angel," he said and laughed again. Then in a very serious voice he asked her to be his wife.

"How can I? You're only a dream."

"Only a dream? A moment ago I was an angel, and now I am only a dream?" For the first time he snapped at her. "I have been here for you since you were twelve years old. I've protected you from your monsters, built you up when the people in your life tore you down. I have loved you in a way no mortal ever could." There was anger in his voice, just enough to make Val leery. Without Luc there would be no life for her.

"I am sorry, Luc. I just don't understand…."

"Well, understand this…" He reached for her, but she was afraid of him and pulled away. This angered him more and he grabbed her, his face reddening. Valerie tried to pull away, but Luc held her firmly. His hands roamed across her body and she tried to fight him. She could not believe what was happening. What Valerie saw next was truly terrifying. Luc began to change: he became larger than before, reddened, with claw-like hands, and a face that would turn one's blood to ice. Her mind reeled as she remembered the monsters of her childhood, the teeth and the claws.

"Luc, short for Lucifer…oh God," she whimpered, then suddenly screamed at him, "You tricked me!"

"Of course. And you were so easy. There were never any monsters, Valerie. It was me!" He laughed. "You are mine. You were always mine. You silly woman. Think of your name! There is EVIL in your first name and your destiny is in your last!" He pulled her to the ground. "My child will come from this union, half mortal, and will live in your world."

"I will kill it!" she threatened.

"You will never have the chance because I will always be with you, as I have been from the beginning — to protect you and the child." The claws dug deeply into her flesh.

When Valerie awakened, the newly born child lay beside her. He was blond and beautiful, his father's son. Just as the paramedics entered her little apartment she started to scream, then went after the baby with hands poised to harm. Strong hands gripped her wrists while another set of hands injected a sedative.

Alone in her little room at the sanatorium, Val rocked back and forth, pitifully making her own noises to block out Luc's laughter from the corner of the room. When Dr. Perkins made his rounds, Valerie pleaded, "Please, oh please, make him go away."

DAN SLOAN

# Day Dreaming

Three weeks ago, I was walking to the corner convenience store. I had a craving for some chili. A bright red 1949 Plymouth pulled up next to me, and the driver lowered the window. I remember the car since no 1949 Plymouth was painted bright red from the factory and the restoration was as close to factory fresh as I had ever seen.

"Say buddy, can you tell me how to get to the Eastside Mall from here?"

"Sure, you just go to the next light and turn right. Then go three blocks and turn left. The Mall is at the end of that street. You'll drive right into the parking lot."

"Hey thanks, may all your dreams come true."

Not thinking any more about the incident, I went ahead, bought my can of chili, and returned home. That was a good bowl of chili. After watching TV for a while I went to bed. Now, when I eat chili for dinner, I tend to have weird dreams. That night was no different. I had a dream about a large cat that lived next door to me. There was a large boxer dog in the neighborhood that had a reputation for being a cat killer. In my dream I saw the cat jump up on the dog's back and ride it like a bucking bronco down the middle of the street.

Now, I don't usually remember my dreams, but for some reason, this one stuck in my mind. I was thinking about the dream when I got home. I stepped out of my car and looked down the street just in time to see the neighbor's cat jump up on the back of the cat killer. With ear-piercing yowls that cat dug in its claws and held on for dear life. As soon as those claws sank into its hide, the dog let out a scream and started running down the middle of the street. I don't think I laughed so hard at anything in years. Then it dawned on me; my dream had just come true.

I didn't remember any dreams for the next two nights. On the third night I dreamed about a car accident at an intersection that I didn't recognize. A taxicab ran into the back of a truck. The truck was lifted up and dropped down on the windshield of the cab. Nobody was hurt, but the fire department had to be called to release the cabby.

The following day I had a call to go across town to pick up some designs from a client. I pulled into a parking lot near the client's office. As I walked towards the building, a very strong feeling of deja vu engulfed me. This was the intersection in my dream. As I stood there, I saw a taxicab run a red light and wedge itself under the back of a delivery truck. The truck was lifted up and crashed down on the cab — right onto the windshield. I turned to a pay phone and called 911. The fire department did have to cut the cabby out of his car. Nobody was hurt, but I was disturbed at having another dream come true.

I remembered a third dream the next night. My secretary is an attractive single woman. In my dream we were talking about something when she came over, picked a dark thread off my shoulder and teased me about having someone leaning on me. Sure enough, after I came back from lunch the next day, I was working on a letter to a client about the design and color of the wallpaper she wanted to use in her hallway; I'm an interior decorator. I frequently consult with my secretary when it comes to color combinations because she has a good sense of color. I happened to be wearing a white shirt that day. As we were talking, she walked over, reached out and picked a black thread off my shoulder.

"Why Jimmy, I didn't know your girlfriend was a brunette, I thought she was a blonde. Who were you having lunch with today?"

"Give me that. Just as I thought! That's not a hair, just a thread from my jacket."

Then I realized: another dream had just come true. The dreams that I remember were starting to come true. I remembered dreaming about winning a free cup of coffee at the local Starbucks when I bought a bagel, and sure enough, the next time I bought a bagel, I got a free cup of coffee to go along with it.

I haven't had a nightmare in years, but last night I had a real screamer. I dreamed that I was up on the top of a very tall building. I was standing near the edge. I was close enough to see down to the street below. The people appeared so small that you could just barely make out what they were wearing. The wind was blowing briskly and I was getting chilled to the bone, just standing there in my shirtsleeves looking down. I heard a loud thrump — thrump — thrump sound coming up from behind me. I turned and saw a news helicopter from a local TV station. The pilot was trying to land it on the roof next to me. Just as he was about to set it down, a big bird, a hawk or eagle, crashed into the rear rotor of the helicopter. There were so many feathers flying around that I could taste the dustiness of them in my mouth. The helicopter started to spin. I jumped down flat onto the roof just in time for the skids under the bubble of the helicopter to skim over my back. One of the skids caught the cornice at the edge of the roof, and the helicopter tipped up and over the edge. I caught a glimpse of the face of the pilot. He was frantic. He couldn't do anything to stop the movement; I saw him realize he was a dead man. The helicopter disappeared over the edge. I jumped up just in time to watch it fall all the way down, landing with a fiery blast in the midst of the mingling crowd down below.

Today I am going to be interviewed by Janice Moore, a newscaster on KKLY TV. They are to send a helicopter to pick me up. I am to meet it on the roof of the building next to my office.

Has anybody seen a red 1949 Plymouth? I need to find it.

JULIE JENNINGS

# For the Sake of Love

He paced his cell for the umpteenth time, his feet dragging across the gray cement floor. Who would've thought that he'd end up here? Seventy years old and in prison.

Griffie leaned his frail body against the cold bars. He'd been in this damn place for six months now, convicted of killing his oldest son and daughter. He didn't want to, really. It was a slow build up, a feeling of lost hope.

Shelton in the next cell, strode towards him. This youngster had made some bad mistakes a few years ago. Still, Shelton was a good chap, always there for Griffie.

"Hey, ol' man, you wanna talk about it? Might help, ya know?"

The boy was right. It wouldn't hurt to get this off his chest. Tears rolled down the charred wrinkles of his face. "You ever heard of the Yankees?"

"Yep."

"My boy played for them." Griffie wiped the tears with his sleeve.

"What did he play?"

"Pitcher."

Shelton whistled long and hard. "The pitcher of the Yankees was him? My dad talked about that guy. So you took him out?"

"Out?" Griffie scratched his bald head. "You mean when he got killed?"

"Yeah."

Griffie clenched his hands around the bars. "Marcus was the apple of my eye. I was his father and buddy. Marcus loved baseball since he was four. Went to every game, put him on the best teams, private lessons and all. My boy played for the minors, the Eagles. One day as I was watched, Marcus picked up the bat, ready to swing and crumpled to the ground. I ran through the crowds."

Shelton squatted on the gray cement floor. "What happened?"

"I was told he'd passed out."

"Was he sick?"

"Doctors said a panic attack. Each game we went to he got worse. A few times his muscles jerked. He lost so many games. Hospital always sent him home. Cared for him until he was well and had that spunk back in his voice."

"Damn. How old was he when this started?"

"Twenty-seven. No one wanted him on the team anymore, not even as a coach. Lost track of time and players."

"What did he do when he was better?"

"Tried to work as a janitor. Couldn't get disability. Blasted hospitals...." Griffie clasped his hands, wringing them together. In all his seventy years, he'd never breathed an odor quite like this. He wrinkled his nose before speaking. "Because the bastards hadn't a diagnosis for him. Said it was all in his head."

"God, that's horrible. You cold?"

"Not cold. It's the memories."

"Still wanna talk?" Shelton hit at a fly that crossed his path.

"S'pose it'll do me good like you said." Griffie felt a shadow of a smile lift onto his face. "I remember Marcus's first game...."

Shelton moved forward inclining an ear toward Griffie.

"I gave him advice."

"What did you tell him?" Shelton smiled encouragingly.

"Don't be too serious, son. Go get 'em buddy and have fun."

"Sage advice if you ask me. Wish I had a father that involved." Shelton frowned.

"He was the cream of the baseball crop until the monster began to eat at him, year by year. I could hardly stand it."

"Didn't you have a daughter too?"

"Two of them, Kelly and Stephanie. Kelly's dead."

Griffie stared through the space between the bars. His sweetheart, Kelly, his princess of life, dead. Oh God, he couldn't stand by and watch her suffer any more than he could watch Marcus. Tears once again poured down his sunken cheeks. Why don't these damn people understand that he did what he had to, for the sake of love? "Kelly was a darling, so motivated, full of life. Best dance teacher on this side of the Rockies. Had her own studio."

"So why kill her?"

"Shelton, you're a young whipper snapper. But I think you might understand my love."

"Go on."

"Kelly had a zest for life even when she was little. Danced well. From the time she was six she wanted to be a dance teacher. Of course, she had to learn to dance first. My wife Cynthia and I went to nearly every performance. I'd take off work to see her shows. What a wonder she was! Then…" Griffie sucked in his breath and shook his head despairingly.

Shelton passed a piece of chocolate to him.

"Thanks." Griffie had learned how special prison treats were. But he also knew things were expected in return. "What do you want me to do?"

"Honestly?"

"Yep."

"You need a friend, ol' man. Just tell me your story."

"I need to back up."

"Go for it." Shelton wiggled in his position but maintained his attention with Griffie.

"Well, she made honor roll. She'd made it despite her mother's death from cancer that year."

"God almighty, Griffie, you shore been through the wringer."

"Back to Kelly and her graduation. She looked so proud in her royal red gown and cap trimmed in blue. She spoke from the pulpit with confidence as valedictorian. 'Live life as if it were ending soon. Meet your goals of childhood, and as an adult empower yourself to the betterment of the world. Let nothing stand in your way.'" Griffie remembered so well. The audience had roared with a standing ovation. His heart had pulsed with love — one of the better moments after the tragedy of his wife. He hated hospitals for poking and prodding, making the wrong diagnosis and taking her from him. God, he really hated the doctors, nurses, and all those who supposedly had such great knowledge in the medical field. "Then she had her dance studio that she'd always dreamed of — at twenty-three."

"Were you happy for her?"

Griffie bit into the chocolate and looked up. "Yes, of course. Wouldn't you?"

"Yeah, but you murdered her."

"Understand, Shelton, that something through the years happened."

"Such as?"

"I'd gone to a dance rehearsal that she had planned for the Pantage's theater in Tacoma. Hard work. Long hours. Then the monster hit her."

"Meaning?"

"Let me tell you. More important to let you know what happened when they got killed."

"I'm all ears." Sheltie wiggled them to prove a point.

Griffie laughed. First time in ages. "You're a card, Shelton."

"Gotcha to smile, didn't I?"

"Yep." He walked around as he spoke. "Kelly forgot the date of her own performance. Wasn't like her. I thought it was due to her work."

"But it wasn't?"

Griffin's shoulders slumped. "No, it was just the beginning. After several months of forgetfulness, my gentle but zestful Kelly became violent."

"Shit. That must have been a shocker."

"Doctors said she was under stress, that's what they called it. Just let her stay on bed rest. Gave her sleeping pills and something for depression. She'd be all right after a few months away from her work, they said. Doctors don't know a damn thing."

"I see where you're comin' from, pops."

"Kelly lost control of her mind and her body. Doctors couldn't figure out what was going on with her. Symptoms started at twenty-six but the medical profession didn't know because it mimics other diseases, but you 'd think they should have got this matter solved. She became a shriveled vegetable. My little girl…" Griffie dabbed at his eyes. "The monster took full hold when she was thirty. I cared for them as infants for twenty-years."

"Try counseling?"

Muscles in Griffie's arms tightened and he clenched his hands. "You think I'm going to trust my family to those people? They're my family and I'm the one who must be responsible. I know my viewpoint on doctors and the medical field now. "

"Counseling could have helped."

"Pshaw! What kinda love would they have for my family?" Griffie sobbed.

Shelton reached through the bars wordlessly and patted his friend's hand.

"I'm sorry. I stood in Marcus's room. He'd shriveled into nothing; his muscles danced. Twenty years like this. The monster had reduced him to nothing. I couldn't bear to see him like this. Marcus deserved peace. I certainly wouldn't like that for my own life, to live it out like a vegetable, with no hope."

Griffie remembered picking up the gun. The cold steel trembled in his hand. At Marcus's bedside, he leaned over and said, "I love you, son." Covering his head with a towel, he stepped back and aimed. The blast of the shot had carried him like the wind against the door, jamming it open. Stunned that it was already done, Griffie looked one more time at his son, now at peace from pain. It was done.

"Did you always have the gun?"

"Yeah, me and Marcus used it for target practice from time to time."

He'd slumped his shoulders and shuffled into Kelly's room, gazing at her dance trophies in the window. "I stared at my Princess curled in the fetal position, weighing no more than ninety pounds at five-foot-six. Her brown hair lay in a sweep against the pillow plumped underneath her head."

A single tear spilled down his face. The monster had eaten two of his children through the years. Yes, it was the right thing to do; he loved her.

"I'm with you, man." Shelton still gripped his hand.

"I moaned and wiped my tears away. I straightened my shoulders, moved to Kelly, stroking her warm cheeks, and kissing her forehead. 'Princess, I love you. I release you from the pain,' I said, then I placed a clean towel over her head…"

Griffie remembered clutching the gun, stepping to the doorway. He'd wiped the sweat from his bald head. "No one should have to live like this. Not anyone, Shelton."

"So you reached the point of no return watching your children shrivel?" Shelton sighed deeply. "Wow."

"One shot through her head. The power of the gun threw me to the ground. My ears turned deaf. It shall be done." Griffie bowed his head.

"I don't understand."

"From the Bible."

Griffie knew he had one more mission to accomplish. And then his children and future grandchildren would be safe from the monster. Stephanie would be coming in soon from work at Porcupine Hill, an elite place where she worked as a maid.

"What happened with Stephanie?"

"She had refused to take a test for the disease. 'When it's time, Dad, but not now.'"

How could he force her to understand, even at thirty-five, that the chromosome monster would either be there for her or her children? More than half of all family members are affected. Made him sick to even think of Stephie, his baby of the family, suffering like the other two. No, it wasn't happening. Sorrow ate his soul. Fear ate his heart. He'd watched Kelly and Marcus disappear through years of care. She should be able to live, but what if the monster got her? He had banged his head against the wall; his mind soared with loss and pain.

Griffie winced as he relived that nightmare. Griffie stood, and moved to the other side of the room with slow steps. "Stephanie entered and stopped, rooted to the spot. 'Oh my God. What have you done, Dad?' I positioned the gun. 'I love you, Stephie.' I cocked the gun. Stephie's blue eyes widened. 'Dad, let's talk this out.' I stepped forward. 'I can't let the monster get you, too.' She moved closer; I'd been too focused on the grief in my heart. 'Give me the gun, Dad. We can get help.' 'I don't need no damn help....'"

"Oh, Griffie. I never knew."

"She says to me, 'Dad, let me help you,' and reached for my gun."

"Then the police came and took me away and here I've been for the last six months, convicted of killing my kids."

"So what really murdered your children?"

Griffie slipped to the floor. "Huntington's."

DAN SLOAN

# The Cure

From the hillside, the valley below looked to be on fire. The rising sun reflecting off the shattered glass made the bombed-out city glow. Carla and Sheri stood on a bluff overlooking the scene. They were on a quest, searching for the family they were separated from when the early warning sounded and they had to evacuate to their mountain sanctuary above Seattle.

The year was 2083; the Chinese had become tired of all the endless nattering from the second-rate West U.S. Confederacy. With the picketing, rioting, and strikes going on all the time, the Central Party would not tolerate further dissention from this province. They had issued a warning about what would happen if one more city held a free election demonstration. Seattlites, as usual, pushed the edges of the envelope. A one-week warning was issued, a three-day warning was delivered, and then the ultimatum was thrown down. The next day the ICBMs fell. There would be no more demonstrations, ever.

Now that the radiation was dissipating, it was time for the survivors to return to try to start over. Carla and Sheri were survivors. They had prepared their sanctuary well in the old cave house near Issaquah, well suited to be the ultimate survival fortress. They added the steel doors and window shutters that had thwarted the looters and gangs for six months. The last attack had been over two weeks earlier. When all became silent, they emerged with full backpacks, rifles and quarterstaffs to see if they could find Aunt Suzy and Uncle Charlie. Suzy and Charlie had been professors at Seattle College until that fatal week. They made sure Carla and Sheri went to Issaquah on time.

As the sun cleared the Cascade Mountains, the two women continued their trek out of the hills. The night before had been filled with the sounds of violence — screams in the night, the roar of motorcycles, and gunfire. The two had the foresight to stay clear of the old roads where the gangs ruled.

"Okay Sheri, let's keep moving. I want to be clear of the gang area before nightfall."

"Just a few minutes more. This scene is breathtaking." Carla stood, shrugged her backpack higher on her back and started to move down the trail. With a sigh Sheri followed. They continued until dusk, stopping then to refill their canteens from a small stream that flowed through a glen. They rested and ate a dinner of trail mix. Sheri was first to spot the house behind the trees.

"Carla, that house may have someone with news about conditions below. Let's take a quick look."

As they got closer, they could see the A-frame was deserted. The door was ajar, and one window was broken with glass shards lying on the ground. The place was a mess; the furniture was scattered; books and papers littered the floor. There was a damp musty smell permeating the place. Sheri climbed to the bedroom in the loft. Carla headed to the back of the house.

"Hey Sheri! The bathroom still works. Now we don't have to imitate the bears."

Outside Carla found the garage, a smokehouse and a root cellar. The garage was empty, but in the smokehouse hung a large ham. Someone still lived there. Where were the occupants? A car maybe? There was a large metal tank hidden behind the garage. Gasoline? The root cellar was spacious. Sparsely stocked shelves and cabinets lined the concrete side walls. The back wall had a series of large hooks mounted high on the wall.

*I wonder what those hooks are for?* thought Carla.

When Carla pulled the cellar door closed, she heard the latch fall. The last person down there had not pulled it all the way shut. Sheri called to Carla, "Let's get out of here. I don't like the feel of this place. It's creepy."

"Yeah, Someone is still living here. Let's clear out now. We can come back later."

The girls walked into the woods and made a cold camp. After sundown they heard the sound of a pickup rattling down the rough driveway to the house. Soon the popping sound of a generator started and lights came on. Carla dug some binoculars out of her backpack and saw two figures moving around.

"Their ba-a-a-ack."

"Don't do that Carla, you know I scare easy. What's going on?" asked Sheri.

"I think the owners are fixing the window. Everything looks benign. We'll go back in the morning. It would be nice to mooch a ride into town," Carla replied.

The night was overcast and too quiet. Complete silence smothered the glen and woods, no animal stirrings, no road sounds. It was as if the world were avoiding the little glen near the house.

The morning fog settled in the glen, shrouding the house. A small plume of wood smoke snaked its way upward through the gray mist. A faint aroma of fresh brewed coffee tempted Sheri and Carla. The chill of the night could be warmed away with the heat of the wood stove in the cabin. Both girls were hungry for something more than another handful of trail mix.

"Carla, do you smell coffee?"

"Yeah, I sure could use a hot cup right now. I wonder how friendly the people in the cabin are. Let's go find out."

The front of the cabin emerged from the mist as the girls drew near. The broken window was covered and the door was closed. They could see only a few yards in each direction. It was as if they were in a chilly bubble, isolated from the rest of all things alive or dead by shifting walls of gray obscurity.

Sheri knocked on the door. No response.

She knocked again. "Hello the house."

A loud and ominous metallic snick-snack sounded behind them as the door latch snapped back and a woman opened the door a crack. The woman said, "Yes?"

A male voice behind Carla and Sheri said, "Slowly lower your rifles and step back towards me."

They set their quarterstaffs and rifles down on the ground in front of the door and slowly backed up.

"That's far enough," said the male voice. "Priscilla, pick 'em up." Priscilla opened the door, stepped out and picked up the rifles. "Okay, go inside," said the man.

Priscilla stepped to one side, opened the rifle bolts, and unloaded the rifles as Carla and Sheri warily stepped over the threshold. The house had been cleaned. Everything was upright. The books and papers were all restored to their rightful places. The room was warm, and the aroma of coffee and ham filled the space.

The door closed behind them. "John, do you think these are the people who trashed the place yesterday?" Priscilla asked.

"I dunno. You two, drop the packs. Who are you and what are you doing here? Don't try anything silly."

As they took off their packs, Carla spoke up. "We are Carla and Sheri Piper. We're heading into Seattle to find some relatives we left behind. We were walking by about dusk last night and saw your place. We camped in the woods nearby. The smell of your coffee tempted us here. We mean no harm. Give us back our rifles and we'll get out of here, now."

"John, I believe her. Put the shotgun down. They don't look threatening," said Priscilla. "Would you and Sheri care to stay for some coffee?"

John ejected the shell from his shotgun and leaned it against the wall where Priscilla had leaned the empty rifles.

"Come over to the table. I just made a fresh pot. John and I were just going to have some breakfast. Would you like to join us?"

John came back to where Carla and Sheri were standing and said, "I'm John Alden and this is my wife Priscilla. We came here from the city when the general strikes started and have been trying to avoid trouble. I apologize for pulling a shotgun on you, but someone broke into our home and trashed it yesterday while we were in the city looking for supplies. We will gladly share what we have. Please sit down."

Priscilla gathered plates, cups and saucers from the kitchen and laid the table. "Yes, John and I have been here for…what…six months? Since the bombs fell. Yesterday was the first time we left the homestead to venture inward. I insisted John take along the Geiger counter. You can't be too careful these days going into the city."

Sheri asked, "Is there anything I can do to help? Where's the silverware?"

"The top drawer next to the sink," said Priscilla. "There are napkins in the top drawer of the hutch. Would you put them on too, please? I'm afraid all we have for breakfast is some fried ham. We did find a Starbucks Coffee Shop that wasn't too badly looted, so we have plenty of coffee."

John sat down at the table next to Carla and asked, "What did you say your name was again?"

"Carla, Carla Piper and she is my sister Sheri. What's it like down in the city?"

"I was surprised," said John. "It looks like there were only three strikes. There's a hot crater where Seattle Center used to be; Mercer Island is gone, and there'll be no more Mariners baseball games. A direct hit in centerfield. There is broken glass everywhere, but no people or animals. The Chinese must have used neutron bombs. Of course the bridges across Lake Washington are sunk, but most of Bellevue and North Seattle are untouched — just completely deserted. It's eerie with no sounds. We didn't stay long. We'll be going back again today to find some canned goods."

Carla brightened, "Hey, if you're going in today, could we get a ride in the back of your pickup?"

"Pickup, how did you know we had a truck?" asked John.

"We were in the woods last night when you drove in," replied Carla.

"Oh, well, I think something can be arranged about that, but let's eat first," said John.

Sheri and Priscilla came out of the kitchen loaded with a platter of ham, bread, and a pot of steaming coffee. They settled next to John and Carla. Sheri poured the coffee and Priscilla passed the ham.

"I hope you like the ham. John and I spent quite awhile cutting and curing the meat ourselves," said Priscilla. "It's our own special cut."

Carla took a large piece, sliced off a chunk and tasted it. "This is sweet for pork," said Carla, "but good. What did you use as a cure?"

Sheri tried a piece and said, "This is really good. You'll have to give us your secret."

John smiled at Priscilla and said, "Have some more. We'll get some fresh meat today and I'll show you how I do it."

Priscilla passed the sugar bowl, and both Sheri and Carla put generous spoonfuls in their coffee.

"Here Priscilla, do you want some sugar?" asked Sheri.

"No thank you. John and I drink our coffee black."

After breakfast Carla and Priscilla cleared the table. John went outside to put gasoline into the truck, and Sheri sat down on the couch in the living room. Sheri was soon fast asleep.

Carla yawned, "Boy, I'm more tired than I thought I was."

"Well, why don't you join your sister on the couch. We'll wake you when it's time," said Priscilla.

Carla sat on the couch, leaned against her sister, and was soon snoring right along.

Priscilla went out back to the garage. "John I'll go open the cellar. It's time to start," she said.

As Priscilla went to the cellar, John started the generator again. He then went inside the house. First he carried Carla down to the cellar, then Sheri. Priscilla tied Carla's wrists together and then Sheri's. John picked up the girls and hung each one from one of the hooks on the back wall of the cellar.

Later that afternoon Carla and Sheri personally found out what the special cure was that John and Priscilla used for their hams.

J. R. CARLSEN

# Relaxing in the Garden

Late one afternoon after I finished my daily drink, I dozed off while relaxing in the garden. As a blanket of leaves blew around me, I woke to grimy hands lifting me right off of my seat. Overpowered, there was no way I could fend them off. How dare they invade my home!

Next, my captors plopped me on a cold table and discussed what they would do to me. Pretending to be asleep, I felt lines drawn on my head. No one uttered a word to me. After that, I felt the first deep cut. They gave me nothing for pain, but each slice numbed me.

They placed a circular section from the top of my head next to me on the table. Tentatively, they probed inside and scooped something out. They scraped and scraped inside my head. Surely, this was my demise. What more could they do to me?

Deep gouges scarred my face. My mouth opened wider. My eyes opened, but I could not see. Something foreign was placed inside my head that brightened my sight and warmed my innards. Then, the top of my head was replaced and they lifted me yet again. They took me back outside—this time to the porch. Several people approached, but they were dressed so strangely. They peered at me and then I heard them chorus, "Trick or Treat!"

# The Tortured Soul

ROBERT HARTLE

A soul is trapped,
Nowhere to go.
Like a room with no windows,
A stairway to oblivion.

Running, running, but nowhere to go,
Looking around, looking here, looking there.
You talk to yourself and get no answers;
When speaking to people, they never listen.

You start screaming inside your mind
While demons inside you say, "Your life's a waste of time."
You look to escape, but you are trapped.
Sooner or later your senility snaps.

You become irrational and look for a *way*,
To end your tortured miserable day.
Thoughts of suicide flash on by;
You give into death, telling life goodbye.

The relatives and friends ask only if
You tell yourself you have tried before,
The person's tortured soul
Is tortured no more.

JULIA COUSINEAU

# Ladonna's Game

**D**eath had cheated her again. She awakes safe in her bed, short of the final splat on the hard ground. "No. No no no! Scum. Liar. Hypocrite!"

LaDonna claws through a sweaty maze of sheets and stumbles into the bathroom. Scalding shower needles impale her skin, granting permission to scream her frustration anew.

So far Death has had her on a building, a cliff, a plane, thin air and, once or twice, no more than a trip on a curb, jolting her awake to Death's scornful laughter licking at her ear. Ever the joker. Flim flam, thank you Ma'am. The ace up Death's sleeve had come to her as a young man named Aaron, with eyes full of summer and a smile she could not bear to be away from. His soft warm kisses were her sustenance.

Many lip-synchs ago, LaDonna's plumage shimmered brighter than the neon on Fremont Street. Sitting in front of her mirror, not ready for another spin on Death's Wheel of Fortune, LaDonna, at this frightening comfortless point in her life, is terrified of what may be staring back. Aaron walks by, giving her the opportunity to grab his hand and hang on — the lifeline pulling her away from what she no longer can be.

"You're so young, you'll slip through my hands like a piece of soap."

"Donny, you look like a kid that's been slapped and doesn't know why. I'm going gambling. Where's the money you owe me from last night?"

"I'd like to crawl into your mind. I can lie next to you, hold you, and still not feel close."

"Get a grip, you pathetic old freak. Good luck getting in on someone else's life. Especially when theirs is moving on and up and yours is, well, pretty much over and down."

"Your restlessness scares me, Aaron."

"I'll call you, Donny. You have to understand." But he never explains.

In a world that knows no day or night, LaDonna waits, stroking the phone as if it were all the good luck charms in the world. If only it would ring, bringing his voice saying that casual flippant "Hi." But no, it is silent, yet speaking louder than his being on the phone himself. LaDonna never thought her entire life would center on a phone, but it does. It does. Because the phone is stickman Death's loaded dice.

LaDonna leaves the suite. Each day's brightness is a painful assault on her. Caught beneath an acrylic blue sky, a faded woman crouches on the sidewalk crying. Farther on, spectral limousines slink past an old man in squeaky shoes — his breakfast, lunch and dinner held in a bag of popcorn. More suckers in Death's casino.

Reaching a broken-down pier, LaDonna walks to its end without hesitation. Aaron will be left with nothing but her outdated wigs and his empty pockets. Death will know she's gone and be furious. You can't please everyone, but she is certainly pleased with herself. After all, isn't she finally hitting the jackpot? Eyes wide open, wide-awake, she jumps.

PATRICIA LAWTON

# I Told You Not To

Ann wondered if it was still there, deep in the recesses of the old trunk. Probably, since she used to tease her mother about never throwing anything away. Opening the trunk, she was assailed by old scents.

She sifted through the memorabilia: an Evening in Paris bottle, old report cards, a plastic hair comb with a date on it, a bank in the shape of a Howard Johnson restaurant, a pressed rose necklace still with a faint scent to it, and a Life magazine with the original astronauts on the cover. All the old memories returned.

But today she was after something different. Reaching through the layers she found it sitting on the bottom. It was cool to the touch as she lifted it out. What a wonderful gift the little green plastic radio had been for a seven-year-old.

Ann's favorite shows had been "Let's Pretend," followed by "Space Patrol." Her imagination always got her involved with the stories. Ann became a participant. She vividly remembered one particular program.

Late one evening, Ann had tuned to something different. Three men were exploring a dark and dank cave. They prepared to descend, one by one, into its depth. Securely anchoring a rope near the entrance, the first man began his descent into the yawning depths. Then from the first man came a terrible scream followed by silence. The second man called out. No response. He started downward to help his friend.

Ann had run to her mother who told her not to listen to the rest of the program. But Ann, ignoring her mother's instructions, returned to listen.

The terrible screaming again started coming from the radio — terrible soul-wrenching sounds. What was happening? What was it? The third man hesitated, gripped with fear. Finally he descended. What he found sent terror through him. His friends had been ripped to shreds. Did he escape the same fate? Ann couldn't remember. What she never forgot was the voice that spoke directly to her from the radio. "I'm coming to get you next."

After the show, Ann had gone to her mother again and held her tight for protection. Ann went to bed and waited that night in the darkness of her bedroom, but the thing from the radio never came.

On occasion as she grew older — whenever she was alone and it was dark — she would look around her room, thinking of the promise. It had been fifty years. Silly how the words stayed with her.

Ann returned to the radio at hand and started to polish the plastic with a cloth. She noticed that the knobs had yellowed with age. She was just ready to plug it in when she thought of the dust inside. As she blew through the side vents, a greenish glow brightened from within. The radio warmed in her hands. It sprang to life.

Then she heard the voice from long ago coming from the radio: "I always keep my promises."

She did not feel the pain at first, but saw the rivulets of blood trickling down her arms. Screams followed — familiar screams from long ago. Ann realized too late that they were coming from her own throat. The pain washed over her. Then silence.

She fell to the floor with the radio still in her hands. The green glowing light from the radio faded as her eyes dimmed.

One last broadcast could be heard as the radio returned to its former coldness.

The final words: "A promise is a promise — and you, the listener, are next!"

JULIA COUSINEAU

# Put a Sock In It!

"You left your wallet on the bathroom counter again." Ethel marched into the kitchen. Pinched between thumb and forefinger was her husband's ragged wallet. She tossed it onto the table.

Ned thought he heard his wife yammering about something. He came out of the bedroom, scratching his ever-growing beer belly. Instead of bacon and eggs, there was a pile of clutter on the kitchen table. None of it looked edible.

"What's this weird junk? Hey, are those my new work socks?"

"Ha! You and work, there's an oxymoron."

"Who's a moron? I'm not the one playing with socks."

"These socks are the start of my new business. I'm going to make and sell sock monkeys for Christmas."

"What the hell are sock monkeys?"

"Cute, little stuffed toys that any kid would love." She showed him a picture.

"Ugly critters. You're wastin' good socks."

"Bea Denton doesn't think so. She ordered three for her grandkids. And she's heading up the Yule Bazaar this year, so I'm guaranteed a good spot. Someone's got to bring money into this house."

"Don't start with me, Ethel. You know I've got a job helping out old Mrs. Denton,"

"And who cleans her monstrosity of a house twice a week? Me, that's who. When are you going to fix things around here?"

"Where's my breakfast?"

"Mr. Big Shot...since you say you're working, am I getting a decent birthday present this year?"

Yeah, he'd like to get her something special all right. How about a nice, 6-foot pine box! An idea was brewing, though, to get Ethel off his back, at least for a good long while. Old lady Denton had lots of pricey jewelry lying around. If a bauble or two turned up AWOL, she'd never know.

"Don't forget to dump the leaves we raked. You promised yesterday it would get done. And you left the shears outside again. I swear, the cliche 'you'd forget your head if it wasn't screwed on,' was made for you."

"Yeah, yeah. What about breakfast?"

"Can you say McDonalds?"

Ned put on his coat and slammed out of the house. Ethel would sing a different tune once she had a gold bracelet dangling from her wrist or a sapphire ring flashing on her pinky. Then he'd get some peace and quiet. Maybe even three squares a day for a week or two.

Fog crept in and kept the thief company on the evening of the bazaar. *Sweet… in and out of Denton's before anyone could yell "Help! I've been robbed!" Just your average run-of-the-mill break-in. Happened every day, everywhere. No suspects caught, in most cases.*

A package wrapped in shiny purple foil created the centerpiece between them. Ethel couldn't take her eyes off it. "When can I open it? The suspense is killing me."

Ned smirked. *Wait till she gets a look inside.* "Okay, go ahead. Unwrap it," he said around a mouthful of strawberry shortcake.

"Oh…oh! Ned, I don't believe what I'm seeing! Is it really mine? Are those real emeralds?" Tears welled in her eyes.

*Figure it would take something like that to make her weep. Greedy nag. What an actress!* The sound of the doorbell intruded on the festivities.

"Great time for one of your nosey friends to drop by."

"It's okay. Nothing can spoil this day. Besides, I can show off my present!"

Ned flung open the door, ready to tell whoever it was to buzz off. Two police officers blocked his view of the street.

"Mr. Ned Murray?"

"Yeah."

"May we step inside?"

Backing away from the door, Ned shot a quick glance over his shoulder.

"What's going on, Ned? Who is it?" Ethel came into the hallway, wrist held out to show off her trinket.

72

"We have a warrant to search the premises for jewelry..." The officer's glance shifted to Ethel's wrist. "...belonging to a Mrs. Beatrice Denton of 241 SW Grove Street."

"What? I was only there doin' a few odd jobs."

The officer walked toward Ethel. "May I see that bracelet?"

"Isn't it gorgeous? A birthday present from my husband."

"I bought it yesterday. Brand new at Fabulous Fakes. Let me get the receipt," Ned said.

"It resembles the description of an item on the list," said the police officer.

"You stupid idiot. I should've known if it wasn't phony, it'd be hot." Fresh tears flowed.

"Shut your yap..." Ned did a double take on the bracelet. "Hey, that's not the one I bought. Those are rubies and diamonds. Where'd you dump the emerald one? What's goin' on?"

"Where were you last night between eight and nine-thirty p.m.?"

"Playin' cards with my buddy, Al. He'll vouch for me." Sweat prickled across Ned's back.

"I was asking your wife. A neighbor of Beatrice Denton saw you leave the bazaar and return later for cleanup, Mrs. Murray."

The second officer showed them a plastic bag. "This partially stuffed sock was found in the broken glass of Mrs. Denton's back door. We suspect it was used to wrap the hand as a cushion."

"That's a work sock. Ned owns at least ten pairs," Ethel said.

"Mrs. Denton stated she purchased several hand-crafted sock monkeys from you. The sock we found matches the tail of Mrs. Denton's toys. Your husband might own the socks but I doubt he stuffs and sews them into monkeys."

Ethel looked like she'd bitten into a rotten nut. "You got that right. Popping beer tabs is his only talent."

"I can't believe you ripped the old lady off and tried to frame me!"

"Put a sock in it, Ned."

"That's your specialty, Ethel." He mimicked her, "I swear you'd forget your head..."

"Shut up! Mr. Big-Talk-Do-Nothing. If you knew how sick I was of you and your cheap crap..."

"You heard her, guys." Relief washed over him. "So long, Ethel! Enjoy the rest of your birthday...Christmas...life! I'll sure be enjoyin' peace on earth."

Ned's laughter followed the police as they began their search.

P. JUNE DIEHL

# Twisted Tales —
# Red Riding Hood

Dear Diary,

I hate going to visit Granny. I hate the woods. Most of all I hate Tom, the lumberjack's son.

My mom said I had to go. This whole thing is her fault. And on top of that, she insisted that I wear that ugly red hooded cape Granny made me. Was this any way to celebrate my fourteenth birthday?

I grabbed the cape and the basket before slamming the front door shut. Mom said I was to take the basket of bread to Granny. Yeah, right. Who does she think I am? Her servant?

Well, I took my time. When I came to the fork in the path, I decided to go for a swim at the cliffs, so I turned left. I heard the giggles long before I arrived. I couldn't believe it! Tom was there with Goldie. How dare he do that to me! I hate him!

Well, it's not my fault. They were the ones sneaking around behind my back. Goldie screamed when she saw me, and grabbed a blanket to hide her naked body. I totally ignored her. I dropped the cape and the basket. The bread rolled out onto the rocks. All I saw was Tom.

I walked right up to him. He tried to talk to me, but the words never made it to my ears. I pushed him hard. He fell. Right into the water below. I didn't even look. I turned toward Goldie, but she ran away, screaming.

That's when I looked back at Tom. He was floating. Face down. Like I said, this is all his fault. And my mom's. What was I supposed to do? The only thing I could. I left. That's right. Just left Tom dead in the water. What did I care? After what he'd done to me? I hope he rots in hell.

So, I picked up the bread, brushed it off, put it back in the basket, and headed toward Granny's.

The cape? Guess I forgot it. It's probably still lying on the rocks. It clashed with my red hair anyway.

It was past dark when I arrived at Granny's. She asked me a thousand questions. I just shrugged my shoulders. It's none of her business. I wanted to leave, but she said she had something for me. Right! Big surprise — a birthday cake. It was chocolate, my favorite, so I said I'd stay to have a piece. The cake was lopsided, but at least it tasted good.

That's when the knock sounded — just as I put a big piece of cake in my mouth. I wiped the chocolate icing from the corner of my mouth and tried to listen.

Granny had answered the door and I could hear two other voices, Tom's dad and the sheriff, Mr. Wolf. Granny was saying something, but I didn't wait to listen. I headed out the kitchen door.

And that's why I hate them all. How could they ruin my birthday like this? To hell with them all. They wanted me to write a confession. There's barely enough light in this dank cell to see anything.

What's the use? Mom'll take my words and God only knows what kind of story she'll twist them into.

Anyway, I leave this "confession" behind. I'm out of here....

— Red

PATRICIA LAWTON

# Fred and Ginger

T he beauty of the fall colors on the hillsides had disappeared.
They had never been in true darkness before. In the city
there was always light everywhere you turned. Even the full
moon didn't help now. The narrow road the couple traveled undu-
lated like a snake, up and down and around corners. Jenny leaned
into Carl, taking hold of his arm, holding tightly.

Looking for a place to spend the night and get some food, they
spotted a sign that read: Littleville — Home of the Best Gourmet
Burgers in the World. They laughed. They were always on a quest
for good burgers.

When they topped a hill this time, they could see lights glowing
in the distance like a beacon. It looked like a mom and pop stop
when they pulled up, small but welcoming.

The proprietors greeted them. "Hi, we're Fred and Ginger," they
said in unison, pointing to some pictures on the wall of themselves
in their youth. They had done a lot of dancing.

Fred was tall and gaunt with a fringe of salt and pepper hair. His
eyes were deepset and darkly circled. Ginger, on the other hand, was
short and plumpish, with rosy cheeks and sparkling blue eyes. Her
once-blonde hair was almost white. The back of the restaurant was a
rest home. The old folks that could, helped out front. They actually
contributed a lot.

"Okay, let's bring on these burgers we've been hearing about,"
said Carl. "We're kind of burger experts."

Fred and Ginger exchanged smiles. Obviously they didn't get a
lot of company this time of the year, because the whole group stood
around the table as Carl and Jenny ate. The burgers were great,

loaded with mushrooms and Swiss cheese. The meat itself was not plain.

It was then that Jenny noticed the unusual necklace Ginger was wearing and commented on it. It seemed to be made of several stainless steel oval disks. Ginger blushed and said that she had designed it herself.

There was a small motel across the way. Carl and Jenny retired for the evening. Jenny took the other half of her burger with her. As they walked across the street, Jenny turned to her husband, "Did you hear that Carl?" Looking up at one of the barred triangular shaped windows, she could see someone clawing at the glass. "Poor soul," she thought. Ginger had said that a lot of the old folks suffered from dementia.

Ginger and Fred prepared to retire also. "We're going to have to do something about Joe soon. He's losing a lot of weight. He's stopped eating."

"Can you blame him?" asked Ginger. "Ever since he opened the freezer and saw Lilly's name on the packages. They were close."

"Well," said Fred. "They're going to be a lot closer. She was a little on the plump side. They should make just the right mix together."

"You know, we're getting pretty popular. What if someone wants to make a franchise?" asked Ginger.

"We'll just have to tell them that small is best and we're not interested," replied Fred. Besides, he thought, the recipe still lacked something. They did their usual twirl outside on the porch. As Fred guided Ginger back through the double doors, he patted her bottom. "Yes, maybe a little Ginger was needed."

The motel was nice enough for the two weary travelers. "You know, Jenny, I just had a thought. Those burgers did taste different. What if they are ground up old folks from the rest home? I wasn't going to tell you," said Carl, "but, I think that the necklace Ginger was wearing is made of pace makers. I thought the disks looked familiar. My grandmother had one."

"If you think you're getting the rest of my burger, Carl, you're wrong." The couple moved to the window to look across at the café. The warmth had left it. Instead, a caricature of it appeared. The full moon had perched atop the old-fashioned chimney, making it seem like a clown's hat. The peaked roof along with the three triangular windows, the open double doors and the square windows of the café resembled a jack-o-lantern of sorts. It glowed from within.

They watched Fred and Ginger dance back through the doors, Fred giving Ginger a friendly pat. With the doors shut, a gaping smile appeared on the jack-o-lantern.

When the lights went off, they looked up at one of the barred windows and saw a tall thin person and a short one leading away the man who earlier had been in such a desperate state. The body slumped, the head down.

"Let's skip breakfast tomorrow. I know it's Halloween and my imagination is working overtime, but still…" Jenny's voice trailed off.

Carl squeezed her hand extra hard. "Yes, let's."

## CHARLOTTE RICHARDS

# A Safe Revenge

I t was a typical April day with a fine misty drizzle slicking the
streets and making driving unpleasant. The weather matched
Joe Hagerty's grim mood. Ignoring the honking horns and
squealing tires, he savagely bulldozed his van through the heavy
traffic on Pacific Avenue. The liquid fire of the bourbon he had just
downed at Gilda's Tavern was beginning to heat his simmering rage
to the boiling point. In his mind he recited the words of the note
Karen had written the day she left.

> *Dear Joe:*
>
> *I haven't had the courage to tell you in person
> that we're through, which is why I'm writing this
> note. You're a really nice guy and I never wanted
> to hurt you. But I can't love you as much as you
> want me to. Now that I've met Scott, I know
> what true love is really like. We plan to get
> married as soon as possible. Please forgive me and
> remember all the good times we had together.*
>
> *Karen*

Every time he thought of Karen's leaving, Joe's head felt as if it
were being tightened in a vise. He wanted to find this Scott SOB
and break every bone in his body. But Karen's best friend swore she
didn't know who Karen's new boyfriend was, only that he was either
a cop or a security guard.

The sudden shrill ring of his cell phone jolted Joe out of his dark
reverie, causing him to swerve abruptly and nearly sideswipe a slow-
moving Honda.

He heard Darla, his office assistant say, "The police dispatcher just called. The narcs have raided a place in the North End and they need a safe opened. They want to know if you can get over there right away."

"Okay, give me the address."

Because Joe was well known as an expert in opening safes, he was often called by various police agencies. If a safe was found during a raid, it had to be opened right away because its contents might be the only grounds for arrest and conviction of the suspects.

The address Darla gave him was in an older residential neighborhood. The place looked deserted, so he drove up the alley behind the house. As soon as he pulled into the alley he could see police cars parked haphazardly up and down its length. He carefully squeezed his van through the narrow lane left by the law enforcement vehicles and pulled up behind the house.

Here there was plenty of activity. He could see a number of men, several in uniform, milling around the garage area. Suspects were being searched and handcuffed in the wake of the recent drug raid.

He sat there for a few minutes, watching, and wondering which of the group was his contact. Except for the uniformed cops, it was difficult to tell the undercover narcotics officers from the criminals. Some of the men wore scruffy blue jeans and dirty Nikes. Others were weighted down with enough gold jewelry to stock Tiffany's.

As he reached into the back of the van for his tool kit, a bearded man wearing a gaudy silk shirt unbuttoned halfway to his navel broke away from the group and hurried up to the van. Heavy gold chains clinked together against his hairy chest. He bore himself with a supremely confident manner that Joe instantly disliked.

"You Joe Hagerty? I'm Lieutenant Somers, head of the Narcotics Task Force."

Joe nodded, masking his surprise at the officer's unconventional dress. "You have a safe that needs opening?"

"Yeah." The lieutenant jerked a thumb toward a number of prisoners who were being handcuffed and shoved none too gently into the waiting police cars.

"We just busted these scumbags. We're positive they were running a crack house here, but so far we haven't found enough evidence to put them away until hell freezes over. We're hoping they stashed it in a safe we found in the garage."

He led the way into the garage and stopped in front of a battered-looking hulk covered with a number of layers of badly scratched gray paint. "Think you can open it?"

Joe turned the handle and slowly rotated the dial. From the way the dial turned, he had a pretty good idea what kind of lock it had.

"It'll take some drilling, but sure, I can get it open for you." He took out his tools and prepared to go to work.

The lieutenant hovered at his shoulder. "We're in a big hurry to book all these prisoners. We don't care how you do it as long as it gets done fast."

Joe felt a surge of irritation, fueled by the bourbon he had drunk. Ignoring the officer, Joe concentrated on boring a hole through the dial ring into the lock case with a high-speed drill. Through the hole he could see the edges of the locking wheels inside. Now came the tedious business of trying to find the right combination. On his first try nothing happened when he pulled the handle. His second try was also fruitless.

Somers was becoming impatient. "Can't you hurry it up a little? We haven't got all day."

A nerve in Joe's cheek began to twitch with hidden anger. His palms itched with the impulse to haul off and punch the lieutenant's hairy face.

"Look, Lieutenant, it takes time to open these things. Now why don't you just leave me alone and let me do my job?"

Somers turned without a word and stalked off, but only as far as a drug dealer's Porsche, where he leaned against the hood and watched.

Once again Joe turned his attention to the safe. "Come on, baby," he muttered. "Third time's the charm." He tried the new combination and yanked on the handle, exhaling with relief when he heard the dull thud of the locking bolts retracting. The heavy safe door slowly swung open.

But instead of the cache of drugs and currency Joe had expected to find, he was faced with still another door, this one of light gauge steel. It had a key-operated lock he couldn't pick. *This must be a really old safe*, he thought. He got a crowbar from his van and was sizing up the lock, trying to decide the best angle of attack, when Somers stopped him. He called to a uniformed policeman who was helping to guard the prisoners, "Hey, Sutton, get me the keys we took from one of those slimeballs."

The sergeant soon returned with a large ring of keys. As the lieutenant tossed the keys to Joe, a heavy medallion on a gold chain slid out from inside his open shirt. Joe stared at the medallion's unusual design, and something suddenly clicked into place in his brain like the locking mechanism of a safe. He forced himself to keep his hand steady as he began inserting each key into the lock. After a lengthy process of trial and error, one of them finally turned.

Joe carefully eased the safe door open a few inches. It was then that he spotted something that shouldn't be there. A bomb!

An innocent-looking, but deadly, black box was attached to the right wall of the safe, toward the front, so that anyone opening the door wide enough would catch the full blast of the explosive charge.

The crack dealer who booby-trapped the safe had wrapped his nasty little calling card in layers of shiny black electrical tape and sealed it with wax. Joe could see a pigtail wire snaking from one end of the box to the inside of the door, where it was held in place by a magnet. A motion detector was ready to prime the charge.

*Clever,* Joe thought. The bomb wasn't designed to explode if the safe was opened slowly and carefully. The motion device would activate only if someone pounded on the door or threw it open quickly.

An ingenious idea came to him in a rush which almost made him dizzy. Taking a deep breath, he cautiously closed the door until the bomb was hidden from view. Then he backed away from the safe, showing no sign of his deadly discovery. Casually strolling over to Somers, he forced a mirthless grin, knowing he could count on the detective's reckless impatience.

"Okay, Lieutenant. Safe's open. It's all yours."

Following the ear-shattering blast, Joe crawled out from under the Porsche where he had taken cover and furtively pocketed a shiny object from the littered floor. After being questioned and released, he hurriedly drove away. Miles from the "accident" scene, he pulled over to the side of the road and withdrew the object he had found. He smiled grimly. It was true that revenge was sweet. Revenge would taste even sweeter when Karen learned what had happened to her precious lover.

The sun finally emerged from the clouds, and he let the sunshine play brightly over the medallion's embossed gold finish. When he bought it, the jeweler told him it was the only one of its kind and that his sweetheart would cherish a gift that was so unique. Joe later had her name engraved on the back in fancy script.

His mouth twisted with bitterness. She must have given it to her lover to help him play-act his role of narcotics kingpin. Well, Scott had acted his last role.

84

Smug with the satisfaction of a job well done, he turned the medallion over to reread the inscription.

The engraving was partially obscured by reddish brown stains. To his horror it read:

To Chris
A Loving Husband and Father
From Gina

# Dream On

## CHARLOTTE RICHARDS

We hope you'll read each gripping tale
Our story spinners tell
And hold your breath on every page
While dream worlds cast their spell.

Perhaps you'll feel an icy chill;
Suppress a frightened start:
The classic fear responses to
The horror author's art.

Or else a mystery writer's clues
May leave you quite perplexed
With bitten nails while wondering
What crime will happen next.

Still other stories may inspire
A sense of love and peace
While words of wisdom soothe your heart
And make your troubles cease.

Whatever genre you prefer,
These pages have them all.
Each story line is guaranteed
To  capture and enthrall.

So, dream on, reader, take the time
To span the universe
In flights of fancy, spinning dreams
In lilting prose or verse.

Regardless if it draws a tear
Or wins a happy smile,
Our grand ability to dream
Makes all our lives worthwhile.

# Dream Visions
## (Inspiration)

*...such stuff as dreams are made on*
*— Shakespeare*

# The Ocean

JULIE JENNINGS

Fiery red, fierce yellows
Brighten blue horizon.
Color spills through the sky,
Heightened waves beat their foam
Against the jagged cliffs.
Salty sea air rushes through,
Grey seagull dives for fish,
Sunset invokes peace,
Settling down for night.

JODI SULLIVAN

# The Sewing Box

E very year near the end of November, Emily began to worry about Christmas. By then Christmas was right around the corner and she rarely had any money saved. This year was no different. It was difficult just paying the bills each month and putting food on the table. She worked hard for the money she earned, but it was never enough.

The girls' dad had left five years before. He left Emily to go on the rodeo circuit and promised he would send money to help raise their daughters — Sarah who was ten and Sissy, twelve. Mike was just not cut out for family life. He had loved them, but their life style seemed to smother him. That was the last time they ever heard from him. Emily had no idea where he was, but she guessed it didn't matter anyhow, except for the fact that the girls missed him. He was never much help financially, even when he was still with them. He was really a sweet guy, but never at all responsible. By now he had probably forgotten all about his wife and their little ones.

Every year, it seemed, Emily had received a windfall at the last minute before Christmas and was able to buy presents to put under the tree. The prior year, on the twentieth of December, she had received a check from the local utility company. They returned her deposit of two hundred dollars because she had shown a pattern of paying her bill on time for twelve consecutive months. "God bless those people at the Power Company!" They had not only kept her house warm and cozy, but they had also provided a tree to decorate, a turkey dinner and presents for the girls. The year before that, it was the guy who ran the stop sign down by the corner market. His insurance company made out a check for one hundred seventy-five dollars, the exact amount of the estimate to fix the rear driver's-side door. Heck, they had three other doors and it was an old car. It didn't much matter if it was dented. The money was better spent on that year's Christmas.

For five years something had always happened to make their Christmas celebration possible. Emily had come to count on it. But this year — now it was December twenty-third — there was no Christmas windfall in sight. It looked like, finally, Sissy and Sarah would know the hard reality of their lives. Santa just wasn't going to stop at their house this year.

Emily went about her evening chores sadly. She started a dinner of scrambled eggs and toast. While she was preparing their meal she looked to see what she could find in her few supplies to make some kind of decent dinner for Christmas night. There wasn't much to work with. There was a bit of ham in the freezer, enough to flavor a pot of soup, a can of cranberry sauce left from Thanksgiving, and a box of corn muffin mix. It would do to fill their bellies. She wouldn't get paid until three days after Christmas. She would just have to make do. Maybe she could fix a special dinner the following week. That would be okay.

After sending the girls to bed, Emily sat down with a cup of tea. She was tired and frustrated. There had to be something under the tree for Sissy and Sarah, even if it was small or made by their mamma's not very crafty hands. Why had she waited so long for a miracle? She had known somehow there would be no miracle this year.

Well, as she had with Christmas dinner, she would just have to make do. Emily went to her sewing box to see if there was anything she could make. At least that was full and well stocked. Her own mother had seen to that. Had her mother really been gone for thirteen years? She had never seen her own beautiful granddaughters. Emily had been pregnant with Sissy the Christmas before her mom passed away. That was the year Emily's mom had given Emily the beautiful antique sewing box which had been her own for so many years. She told Emily to use the sewing box for the granddaughter she would never know.

The box was full of colored threads and yarns, embroidery floss, needles and hooks, buttons and beeswax. Emily had always felt a bit guilty because she had never really sewn for the girls as her mom had for her. Oh sure, she had sewn up rips and tears, replaced missing buttons and the like, but she had never created anything. Emily remembered her mother making lacy party dresses and soft, warm, hooded sweaters. She even made a rag doll with a wonderful wardrobe and long yarn braids. She wished her daughters could have had those kinds of memories. Her own mother had been home all day while her father had supported them. Emily worked long hours and it seemed like she was always tired.

Then Emily had an idea. She would need two identical boxes. Those high-heeled shoes she used to wear would do just as well in a plastic bag. The shoeboxes would be perfect.

Emily stayed up all night. The girls slept soundly while she worked. By morning, when there were two wrapped packages under the tree, Emily slept for a while. Thank goodness she had Christmas Eve day off. When she woke, she heard voices in the living room as Sissy and Sarah circled the tree and discussed what could be in the packages. They looked happy. When they saw her, they asked if Grandpa would be well enough to have Christmas with them this year. Emily's father lived in an Alzheimer's nursing home and was not always able to visit. She called the home and found that his new medication was working well and he wanted to come. She picked him up that night and he slept on the couch.

Emily woke on Christmas morning to the soft knock of her father's hand upon her bedroom door. It was morning and the girls were up and waiting. She put on her old flannel robe and slippers, then followed her dad to the front room. The girls were sitting near the tree, each with a box in their lap. Emily smiled and nodded at them. Both girls started tearing paper and throwing it behind them. Inside they each found a beautifully decorated shoebox. The boxes were lined with quilted satin fabric and had satin-covered cardboard dividers. A small pillow filled with pins and needles was sewn to the side of each box. There were rows of colored threads and yarns, embroidery thread, needles and hooks, buttons and beeswax. With each box there was a note. "These wonderful supplies are from your grandmother, but the time it will take to teach you how to use them is from me. I love you. Mama." The girls were excited and wanted to start right then.

Emily got cups of hot chocolate for the girls and coffee for herself and her father. She showed the girls how to put stitches on knitting needles and how to knit a few rows, and how to purl. They made little squares and cast off. Then she taught them a few embroidery stitches. Sissy noticed that the buttons in her box were like the ones she had played with as a little child. Em's father quietly watched the proceedings, smiling his approval. At one point he mouthed the words, "Mom would be proud of you today."

By mid afternoon the girls had gone to their room with their boxes. The pot of split pea soup was cooking on the stove and the house smelled like a holiday. Emily had just put the corn muffins into the oven when the girls came into the kitchen and told her that there were packages under the tree for her and Grandpa. Sure enough, two soft, brightly wrapped gifts lay under the tree. Emily handed one to her father, and together they opened them. Each held a soft woolen scarf. One was striped and the other had tassels on the ends. With each scarf was a note which read, "These will keep you warm when it is cold out. This has been the best Christmas ever! We love you! Sissy and Sarah."

Tears came to Emily's eyes. This year's miracle had come after all.

DONNA ANDERSON

# The Gift

I love gifts. Giving and getting. I shop all year long for Christmas, and I cruise catalogs, searching for that perfect thing. But the best gift I can imagine for anyone is the gift of friendship and I want to recommend giving yourself such a gift. The gift of a best friend.

I am so lucky to have many friends and lots of acquaintances who are potential friends, but I have given myself the gift of two wonderful best friends. These two have been close friends since my childhood days — I mean very close in my heart, not in miles.

One lives almost four hundred miles away and the other three thousand miles. The closeness I feel is like one feels for a family member. No matter how far apart in distance, they are still a part of my world.

These two friends are from high school. To some that wouldn't seem like a childhood time, but I was a teenager in the 1950s and that was such an innocent time by today's standards. I think of us still as children. The three of us see each other very seldom. Once a year would be nice, but that is not usually the case.

My friend who lives the farthest away is in Canada. She recently had a bout with cancer that we are all praying is under control. So far, so good. We keep in touch via e-mail and letters at Christmas and perhaps a few other letters during the year — and sometimes, a very lengthy phone call.

Just this week she sent me a picture of the three of us taken at her mother's house about fifteen years ago. Our appearances have changed since then, but our friendship hasn't.

The same with my friend who lives four hundred miles away. Total support is just a phone call away. I see her more often because she lives in the town we all grew up in. I visit relatives there a couple of time a year and phone or see her while I am in town. Her latest challenge has been moving her father to an assisted living home. Sometimes the only help you can give is to listen, but we are always available for each other.

Closeness doesn't mean daily contact, although that would be wonderful. It is that secure feeling of knowing at any time that you have a special someone available to help. Moral support is greatly under-rated. Just knowing I can call on either of my friends with my worry or problem, or that we can visit when we want, is as secure as a child/mother connection. We all share true friendship.

What makes these friendships last? I'm not sure. It could be because we truly like each other. It could be we trust each other with our innermost thoughts. It could be we have a track record of caring about each other. It's probably a combination of all of these things. It's as hard to define as love, but I think it is a form of love — true love.

These friends have seen me through happy times and bumpy times, and when we get together we talk non-stop, just like old times. No time barrier here.

If 1 could give my children, family and friends just one gift, it would be for them to have at least one true friendship that would carry on throughout their life. Since this is really a gift only they can give themselves, my wish is that they already have this friend and have the support and love I have experienced. And I do know this: If you can find that special person, a special benefit is the gift of yourself you can give in return.

PATRICIA LAWTON

# The Safe Place

The first thing she noticed was the wood stove. It allowed a fire within but you could not see the flame. The glass was marred from having the fire too hot at one time. The walls were made of rich wood. The colors of the carpet and the furniture were warm earth tones. He sat in the corner of the couch; she sat in the second place next to him. She felt safe and secure. He always made her a pot of tea sweetened just right, always hot enough.

It was here that their two souls met. But one day she came and the couch had been moved across the room. Now it faced opposite. He sat in the other corner. Something was wrong. She sat in the chair next to the couch. She could not seem to find her way back next to him. Usually he would be standing by the kitchen window smoking his cigarette and thinking about — she knew not what. Eventually she gave back the key to the safe place.

She returned to her home and threw herself into making it warm and inviting. It had two fireplaces and a wonderful hot tub to soak in after a hard day. There were plenty of pillows and soft throws on the couch. But he didn't want to come to her home. She sat in the chair by the window, waiting, drinking tea that had no meaning.

She remembered another safe place she had been offered years before. It had three fireplaces. One was so huge that it looked like it belonged in a ski lodge. Gigantic windows looked out upon a beautiful mountain with a river rushing by at the foot of it. A picture-perfect pasture filled the space between the river and the palatial house, surrounded by a split rail fence to protect horses that romped playfully.

She returned to it. The owner now offered her all this and more. It was what dreams were made of. He served her tea also. It was lukewarm, had a strange flavor, and he didn't sweeten it. He had the property and riches most people only dream about, including gold mines in far off places. But, of course, there would be a price to pay. She must forget about the first safe place, for he could protect her much better here.

Despite all that was offered, she was deeply saddened. She knew you cannot buy love with all the riches in the world. It is a gift freely given from the heart. And in her heart of hearts, she longed to return to the safe place on the couch.

Ten years later: If you go by the palatial house, no fire glows from within, for only bought souls live there.

At her place, a gym set stands in the yard, children play, flowers grow. She is not there. They say she died of a broken heart. However, there is a story that if you drive by slowly in the evening on a winter night you can see her sitting in a chair by the window, a fire glowing from the fireplace, and in her hand she holds a cup of hot tea to warm her heart.

And he — well, if you drive by his safe place, you will see him standing by the kitchen window smoking his cigarette. Thinking...

# Touched By An Angel

K aren walked through the open wrought iron gates and paused for a few seconds while she tried to get her emotions under control. She looked down at the bouquet of daisies she held in her burn-scarred hands and could feel the quick sting of tears. Hastily brushing them away, she walked down a long grassy aisle until she came to a headstone with the inscription:

IN MEMORY OF
Daisy Farrell
Born May 17, 1935
Joined the angels
November 8, 1999

Kneeling down on the grass, Karen placed the flowers in front of the tombstone. Then she held up a letter with a New York postmark. "I did it, Daisy! I did it! Thanks to you, I sold my very first novel!"

Karen had met Daisy during an abrupt encounter at Logan College. Late for her evening class, Karen literally ran into Daisy as she dashed down the hall. Accepting Karen's apologies for toppling her over, she said, "You're forgiven. However, if you'd like to meet me at the College Cafe after class, I'll let you buy me a cup of tea to make up for ruining my best pair of panty hose." After brief introductions, they both hurried to their respective classes.

After class, Karen met Daisy at the popular college hangout. While Daisy sipped her tea, she inspected Karen over the rim of her cup. "Tell me about yourself. Besides the opportunity to run down hapless instructors, why are you taking evening classes at Logan?"

Karen smiled at Daisy's humor. "My mother and I were very close because my father was killed in a plane crash when I was a child and she had to raise me alone. After she died and my husband left me for another woman, I had a difficult time coping with my loss. I decided it was time to begin a new life. So I moved to the West Coast and got a job to help pay for my last year of college."

When Karen confessed that she had also been working on a novel, Daisy, who taught advanced writing courses at Logan, became her mentor. They soon developed a close bond. Daisy regarded Karen as the daughter she never had, while Daisy filled the deep void in Karen's life that had opened after her mother died and her husband abandoned her. Karen began to love Daisy as much as her own mother.

Then one day at lunch, Daisy reluctantly told Karen that she had been diagnosed with cancer. In the next few months, the disease progressed so rapidly that Daisy had to be hospitalized. Karen was heartsick to see her dear friend slowly losing her tenacious grip on life.

When visiting Daisy one afternoon she completely lost control and began sobbing, "Oh, Daisy, I don't want you to leave me! My life won't be the same without you!"

Daisy smiled in spite of her pain and squeezed Karen's hand. "You know I'll never leave you. My body might not be here, but my spirit will be watching out for you wherever I am. I promise, if you're ever in trouble or danger, I'll ask one of God's angels to look after you."

Daisy had been dead six months. At work Karen could put her friend's death out of her mind. And while she was in class she could push it away. But it was in the dark still of the night that her grief became overwhelming. She thought bitterly that it wasn't fair that she should lose her mother and her surrogate mother, too. In an effort to deaden the pain, she spent every spare moment working on the novel Daisy had urged her to finish.

Completely engrossed in the development of the characters as she worked late one night on her manuscript, Karen was startled by an explosion that rocked the apartment building. In rapid succession she heard the loud clamor of fire alarms, then screams of panic. She rushed to her door and opened it as a second blast sent dense clouds of smoke and red tongues of fire billowing into the hall. Before she could shut the door, flames licked over her face and hands, singeing her eyebrows and setting the ends of her hair on fire. In a frenzy of terror, she beat out the flames and slammed the door. She stumbled to the window on trembling legs and finally managed to raise the sash with her painfully blistered hands.

But when she looked out over the front courtyard, she realized there was no escape that way. Her apartment was on the fourth floor and the fire escapes were located at each end of the building. She was trapped!

She could hear shouts from people on the ground who had seen her at the window. "Hold on as long as you can! We've called the fire department! The trucks should be here any minute!"

As she heard the distant wail of sirens, she could feel the scorching heat of the fire as it began to burn its way through her apartment wall. She tried desperately to avoid breathing in the acrid smoke. *Oh, Daisy*, she thought in despair, *you said you'd help me if I was ever in danger. Where is the angel you promised to send?*

She swung one leg over the windowsill, gulped in the fresh outside air, and prayed that the fire engines would arrive before the flames reached her.

A chorus of voices immediately reached her ears. "Don't jump! Don't jump! The fire trucks are coming!"

Invigorated by fresh oxygen from the open window, the flames suddenly roared up ceiling high. The crowd gasped in collective horror. In a desperate attempt to escape the searing heat, Karen swung her other leg over the sill and perched precariously on the edge. She debated in terror whether it was better to burn to death or be killed in a four-story fall.

Then a clear voice arose in the midst of the clamor. "Quick, do what I say! Turn around facing the building. Hold on to the window ledge and extend your right foot down as far as you can. There's some decorative stonework down the side of the building. All you have to do is use it for a ladder to get down."

Karen painfully turned her body around and hung onto the windowsill with her scraped and bloody hands. Frantically she reached for the first stone block with her foot. She had almost reached it when a sudden whoosh of flames erupted from the open window and caused her to lose her grip on the window ledge. Another gasp of horror rose up from the crowd. She slid down the side of the building, certain she was falling to her death, but managed to hang on to one of the stones.

"Don't panic! You're doing great! There's a window ledge right below you. Feel around with your feet until you find it. Okay, now reach down with your left foot for another stone."

The voice had talked Karen halfway down by the time the fire trucks came shrieking into the courtyard. A ladder swiftly swung into position, then a sturdy fireman gently plucked her from the face of the building.

Karen awoke, swathed in bandages and reeking of burn ointment and antiseptic. Judging from the metal bed frame and the white curtains partially drawn around her bed, she knew she was in a hospital. Painfully she tried to focus her smoke-blurred eyes, then became aware of someone sitting in a chair beside her bed.

Her visitor smiled warmly at Karen. "Hello! Glad to see you're awake. Hope you're feeling much better after your frightening experience."

Karen tried to smile back, but it hurt too much. The voice was familiar. Where had she heard it before?

Suddenly the trauma-induced fog in her brain cleared. Of course! It was her savior—the person who had persuaded her to make that insane climb down the side of the building.

Her throat still raw from smoke fumes, Karen croaked hoarsely, "How can I ever thank you? You saved my life. But how did you happen to be right there when the building started burning?"

"I was driving down the street when I saw a crowd of people milling around in front. Something told me to stop and see if I could be of any help. Then I saw you at the window and knew I had to get you down fast because the fire would reach you before the firemen could. I later heard that a meth lab exploded in the apartment across the hall from you. That's why the fire spread so rapidly."

Karen looked more closely at her visitor. "I've seen you somewhere before." Recognition dawned. "On TV, that's it! Aren't you Deborah Zeigler? The famous mountain climber? I saw you on the news climbing a mountain in Nepal. No wonder you knew how to talk me down from a fourth-story window."

The woman flashed a self-deprecating grin. "Yes, that's me. Deborah Anne Zeigler." She reached over and gently patted one of Karen's thickly bandaged hands. "But I hate the name Deborah, so all my really good friends call me Daisy." In response to Karen's surprised and puzzled expression, she added, "For my initials. You know—DAZ."

It must have been a slight breeze from the open window, but for one brief moment she felt as if an angel wing had fluttered by and lightly brushed her cheek.

# Day Dreams
## (Nostalgia)

*I thank you for your voices: thank you,*
*Your most sweet voices.*
*— Shakespeare*

# "¿Dònde Estàn Tus Cuentos?"
# ("Where Are Your Stories?")

### Janelle Meraz Hooper

I listened to stories on my grandmother's knee
Stories of coming to a new country,
Stories of courage, living, and strife.

I listened to stories at my mother's feet
Stories of leaving home,
Stories of lust and men and being a wife.

I listened to stories by my father's bed
Stories of growing up in Texas,
Stories of homesteads, ranches and war.

I listened to stories in my neighbor's swing
Stories of childhood and getting by,
Stories of success and failure and more.

I listened to stories from an old man
Stories of the West, and Indians,
Stories of cowboys, and skies of blue.

I listened to them all and remember all
Stories that fill my head and
Now I share them with you.

"¿Dònde estàn tus cuentos?"
("Where are your stories?")
Share them with me and I will listen
Until the stars come out —

JANELLE MERAZ HOOPER

# The Red Plaid Lunch Box

The last time I browsed the antique shops, I came across a red plaid metal lunch box with a matching red plaid Thermos from the '50s. It brought back a flood of memories because I had one just like it when I was in third grade living in the middle of Oklahoma. When I took it off the shelf and opened it, the smell of waxed paper and tuna fish still lingered.

Mom was barely hanging on when I had mine. A victim of a previous violent marriage, family politics, and physical disabilities, she was like a beautiful autumn leaf caught in a storm drain, spinning around and around in treacherous whirlpools — but never going down. I knew she loved me. There was never any doubt about that, but she could barely care for herself, much less take care of me.

My father and stepmother lived across town. I always had the option to go and live with them. They were both employed and the meals were regular. Even if I had wanted to live with them — which I definitely didn't — how could I have left my mom? It wouldn't have taken a Whiz Kid to know that Grandmother and the rest of the family would pick her to death if I weren't there to protect her.

One step above homeless, Mom and I bumped around from one relative's home to another. Our latest move was to the home of my grandmother. Before the lunch box, Mom didn't wake up before I left for school. My grandmother told me that she seldom bothered to get up before eleven-thirty or so. Mom's sleeping habits meant that sometimes I not only went without lunch, but without breakfast, unless my grandmother shared some of hers. Nowadays doctors might say Mom suffered from depression. I've often wondered.

I don't know why things got better for a while during my third grade, but one day I came home and saw that little red lunch box on the counter. I was mesmerized by the shiny exterior and the clean white interior—the way the Thermos fit in just so.

The next morning, Mom was up bright and early wrapping little food treasures in wax paper. A sandwich. Celery. Carrots. Half an apple. Mom was never much of a baker, but a few times I'd find a cupcake made from one of those mixes that used to cost a dime a box.

The little metal lunch box became a barometer of my mother's mental health. If I carried it to school, I knew that Mom was going to have a good day. I carried more than food in that metal container. It was a contract — a contract that said Mom was going to be there, really there, for the rest of the day at least. When I got home after school, she'd be dressed and smiling.

I remember that she made a little bit of money sewing for rich people that year. She was developing a list of clients and was excited about it. Mom sewed beautifully, but her customers never stuck around very long. I never knew why. Still don't.

During that third grade, there were days when I'd come home to find she'd taken the bus to town, and the top of my cot would be decorated with a cluster of new panties, socks and hair barrettes. All of the purchases were probably paid for with her earnings from sewing. The only other money we had was an Army allotment of seventy-five dollars a month from my father. Most of it my mom turned over to my grandmother every month for food and rent.

That year, sometimes I'd go into the kitchen and the red container would be on top of the refrigerator, empty. I could have filled it myself, but I never had the heart. Before I left, I'd go into Mom's bedroom just to assure myself that she was still breathing.

A lot of Mom's life must have been hell. On her bad days she'd tell me the family circled around her while I was gone and picked at all of her flaws like vultures on a dead rabbit. She said they'd carp, "Why can't you get yourself together?" "Why do you sleep so much?" "Why aren't you married?" "Why don't you get a job?" "Why don't you fix up, do your hair?" It got to where I didn't want to go to school when she was still in bed. Once I got there, I couldn't concentrate on what was on the blackboard.

I must have been hungry on those days that I had no lunch, and sometimes no breakfast, but I don't recall. I just remember looking at the clock with my hands folded on top of my desk while my classmates ate, wondering if I had time to run home and check on Mom. Should I go home? What would I find if I did? I'd seen my mother curled up on her bed in the middle of the day so many times I didn't need to see it again to refresh my memory. Even if I succeeded in dragging her out of bed, I knew she'd go right back after I left. I'd sit at my desk and worry about what I should do, until lunchtime would run out and it would be too late to make the round trip. I couldn't call her because Mom was almost totally deaf; she couldn't hear over the phone.

Mom had some happy years after I married and started college. The two of us had moved out of the state by then. She got a job as an alteration lady in a big department store and I worked in retail sales when I wasn't in school.

After I married, the three of us — Mom, my husband, and I — pooled our money and rented a two-bedroom house. During that time Mom blossomed and I don't think I ever made it to the coffee-pot in the morning before she did. My husband left early for school, so Mom and I used to catch the bus to work, and we'd laugh all the way. Then we'd meet for lunch and laugh some more. We lived happily together for over five years before Mom got dragged back home to take care of my aging grandmother.

Two years later, when I went back to visit her, I was shocked at how despondent she had become. I'd almost forgotten the way things used to be when I was young. One quiet night I found myself in the kitchen digging through the cupboards to see if I could find the little red container with the bright red plastic handle, but it was nowhere in sight. I never saw it again, and Mom slipped backwards into her old melancholy life.

Mom has been gone for several years now, a victim of a car accident. I can't help feeling she never had a chance. For years I've wondered why I didn't help her more. I've only begun to realize that beautiful leaf wasn't alone in the storm drain. I was in it too, in those early days. We were both swirling around and around, too helpless to find a way out.

Other than when we left Oklahoma, the closest we ever came to being happy was when she bought that lunch box. I can still remember the way her eyes would shine when she'd hand it to me before I went out the door.

I miss my mother every day. She may not have been the perfect parent that you see on TV sitcoms, but she had some spectacular moments as a mom. I'll never forget the dresses she made for me that were more beautiful than the ones the rich girls had, the trendy swimsuits she fashioned for me out of scraps of material, or the knack she had for making chores fun. There is no doubt in my mind that she tried very hard to be a good mom when she had the strength.

Lately, that little red plaid lunch box that connected us during my third grade year has been on my mind. I might go back and buy the one at the antique store downtown. There's a place for it on my kitchen counter. I think I'll fill it with neat little folded squares of wax paper and put a beautiful autumn leaf in it. Maybe two autumn leaves—I wouldn't want her to get lonely.

ALINE LESAGE

# On Folly Road

I t's stifling hot. The ruts of the narrow dirt road are still filled with water from last night's rainfall, and a faint smell of rot hangs in the air. As I walk farther down the dead-end street, I hear a child crying behind the weathered shutters of a small house. Perhaps *hut* would be a better word for this kind of dwelling, nothing more than a room with an electrical outlet and a pipe somewhere out back.

Though the few people I meet along the way give a polite smile, I am again overcome with an odd sense of discomfort before this, my beloved Jamaica. Farther down the road, a small crowd of women, children and one man are watching "General Hospital;" they all stand one next to the other, engrossed before a television set that was moved to a small verandah for the occasion. They are religiously silent, as if attending a church service. Which it is, in a way. An efficient diversion can be made into a religious act when the plight of daily life becomes unbearable.

I walk by this makeshift group and they hardly notice me, although they should. No *whitie* remains unnoticed in these parts, but then I am of the non-threatening kind: my clothes are plain, I wear no jewelry and I know the ways. I know where to look — not to look — how to nod. And I can speak some fair patois too, which for some reason causes my Jamaican friends to laugh heartily every time.

A scraggly cat walks by as a small child hides behind an old wire fence. His face is dirty and he wears no shoes. He stares at me and I try to smile, but since I am a *whitie*, he quickly turns away and runs towards his mother's cabin.

I am approaching the dead-end of the dusty street now and turn left into an uneven pile of rocks along a few cabins towards Angela's house. Angela is my sister-in-law, and hers is not a real house of course. It's a small, plain cabin with a single separation inside, making it into two rooms. Here she lives with her two teenage sons and a baby grandchild.

As I have seen her do so often, my sister-in-law is hanging her laundry to dry on a makeshift clothesline away from the sun. The sun here can easily destroy all fibers and burn color out of even the best clothing. With a half dozen clothespins in her mouth, she notices me and greets me with her eyes as she forces herself not to laugh. I seem to make her laugh. Or maybe I make her happy, I don't know. After the last pin is finally retrieved from her mouth, I notice that she is not wearing her teeth and I start making a fuss because it makes her look like an old woman. She laughs again; she doesn't care. Then in a singing voice, she says: "Okay, okay, let me do someting for you!" and she steps inside. A few seconds later she reappears, her teeth and her smile properly restored. Now we can talk.

"Whappen?" she asks, as I give her a tight hug that makes her slightly uneasy. She never got used to my openly affectionate French-Canadian hugs, but I make her.

"Be civilized," I tell her. "And don't you know that hugs are good for you?" Angela's face is quite dark, yet I notice a blush on her upper cheeks — the discomfort of our impossible difference. We have been doing this for years now: I tell her she's all wrong, and she tells me she can't understand why I "worry so much about tings."

But I love her dearly, and I think she loves me too. We step inside her living-dining-bedroom. It's the size of my own bathroom, way up north where I come from, where we are civilized and where we have hot water any time we want it. The small table is bare except for a chipped ashtray. The old boarded floor crackles loudly and I can see the dark ground between the wide, discolored planks. A mouse suddenly appears by the curtained entrance to the kitchen and I let out a faint scream, instinctively climbing onto my chair.

Angela giggles as she watches me. I do this every time. "Those godforsaken mice! Can't you do something about them, Angela?"

She laughs again. "You civilized people want to fix everything," she says. "It's not going to kill you!" Now she pulls out two half-crushed cigarettes from her jeans pocket and hands me one. She lights mine, then hers with a hot pink plastic lighter, the only bright item visible in these shabby, yet impeccably clean quarters. It was right here that, contrary to my mother's teaching, I finally learned a few years ago that poverty is not a synonym of uncleanliness and that poor people can be very clean. Don't believe everything your mother taught you.

We smoke, and she stares at me in silence. It's been a year since we saw each other and she feels a need to evaluate me. She studies my hairdo. Then her eyes wander downwards and I know what she's going to say next. "You should lose weight," she comments in her serious voice.

"I love you too," I reply. She understands the message, and takes another puff.

I'm sitting next to a makeshift window, a mere square opening onto the yard, onto the pipe (otherwise called shower) and the shithouse, all shared by a few neighbors. Oddly, if I stretch my eyes towards the left across a jungle of palm trees and banana trees, I can get a glimpse of the real Caribbean Sea, turquoise and alive with tall, foamy waves. The Great Paradox hits me again. Between the glossy travel brochures and the simplicity of Angela's lifestyle — and so many like her — I have learned the immeasurable gap, the irreconcilable differences between two worlds. Still, we pretend. A game we both knowingly play.

Angela sighs gently and looks ahead of her, towards something I can't see. "Money a problaim, y'know…money a big problaim…." Slowly her life unfolds. She tells me about her debts, how she manages to repay some by doing favors for friends. I know what that means and it breaks my heart to see a gifted woman resorting to these sad means. She butts her cigarette out, squishes it in the ashtray. She doesn't look at me now; she can't. I know it's because she is ashamed and sad. I know her pain for not having gone to nursing school because there was no money, because nobody could afford it. I know the compromises she made just to get by, like marrying the first candidate, a man she didn't love, yet who seemingly guaranteed her an acceptable livelihood. That's what counted then, that guarantee. Of course, she was tricked into the web of human frailties, only to find herself — a few short years later — alone with three small children. Her guarantee had fled to America towards a better life, never to be heard from again. That's how it often starts here, the vicious circle of naive hopes and a first class ticket to deception.

Today, of course, Angela is a different woman. Very different. Those guarantees, let alone romantic love, are a laugh to her now. Each woman for herself, she says. That's why she walks around with a knife stuck inside her jeans at all times, snug against her black tummy. That's why the sweet sparkle vanished from her eyes, from the eyes of this once promising and ambitious girl.

The small room goes silent again, filled with faint echoes of playing children and barking dogs. The sultry afternoon is becoming unbearable. I wish Angela had an electric fan and I'm dying for a glass of iced tea or something. But Angela doesn't have a glass of iced tea or something. She has nothing. So I'd better learn to stop wanting — while I'm here anyway — the same way she did, long ago. Because if you foolishly keep dreaming the American dream, you might just go crazy, lose your mind.

Perhaps that's why so many Jamaicans are given to violence. From wanting the impossible and constantly failing, something eventually snaps. Of course, this violent minority only makes a sad and unfair reputation for an otherwise good people. An ultimate Catch 22, a deadly mix of complex economics, corporate greed and institutionalized corruption, all condoning the miserable Gap. But Angela doesn't care much about fancy intellectual explanations. She wants to eat and pay the rent.

As usual when this subject comes up, I too become uneasy because there is nothing to say. After many years of Jamaican exposure, my naive list of suggestions for improvements has long been exhausted. I sigh. I feel guilty over my Canadian passport, scholarly degrees, safe employment, health insurance, and too many luxuries, my children's opportunities that Angela's will never have. The plight rolls from one generation to the next, with too little change in between. I feel depressed. What am I doing here? I want to go home, hide under my Ralph Lauren sheets and reflect on what my life is all about. It's been fourteen years and I feel this way every time.

So perhaps I should do just that, go home. I am ashamed to have once thought that I might have something useful to teach my sister-in-law. Happily, my arrogance died and I know better now: she is the

110

one able to tell me where it all starts and, in the end, what really counts.

Timidly, she asks if I have "a twenty dalla."

"Maybe," I say, waiting to hear what she wants to buy.

She rises from her chair. "All right, so let's get a drink by da road."

Angela slips into her old laceless sneakers, checks her bra, and shows me towards the door. She smiles and looks at me straight in the eyes. "You really should lose weight, y'know!"

I smile back. "Yes, I know."

As we walk together up Folly Road, I don't feel so depressed anymore.

## J. Oden Dock

# Memories of a Boy's Walk

I was sitting in stalled traffic irritated by the monotony of staring at the stopped car in front. But then, if the traffic were moving, I would still only look at the car in front of me, because that is  what I now do as an adult. When I was ten or eleven years old, at that stage of life, I was observant of what was at my left, at my right and at my feet. At that stage I wondered "Why? Why is there grass here? Why are there small rocks there?" At that stage I imagined what happened yesterday to place boulders there.

As I sat, I began to think in iambic, similar to the meter that matched my footsteps which took me on a walk years ago. The walk began at the bottom of a bluff where this boy wondered, "What is up on the top of the bluff where this creek begins?"

Along the Mississippi bank
    the bluff rose up three hundred feet.
And at its base a dry creek bed
    held only pools so still and calm,
But high creek banks gave forceful proof
    of rushing storms on other days.
I went in search of that creek's source
    in quiet meadows high above.

There only flowers first were seen
    upon a level grassy lea.
But to the north the grass was clumped
    with space between for rain to flow,
Then more bare ground between the clumps
    where former flows increased their speed
And rushed ahead to steep'ning ground.
    There tearing soil from grass's roots
'Til grass itself was torn away
    and only stones remained in place.

As I went down the steep'ning slope,
    where swirls had cut a deeper creek,
The banks were soon above my waist,
    and trees stood high on left and right.
Ahead and downward led this creek
    to where the banks were eight feet high,
And roots of trees hung uselessly
    above the rocks of this dry creek.

The scene below was yet more fierce,
    for waters' force had grown more strong.
There in my path an oak tree lay,
    its mighty roots had given way.
Here only boulders had withstood
    the torrent and the violence.

My walk continued downward to
    a scene of nature's other mood.
The dry creek bed of rocks and logs
    became less steep and ponds appeared.
The high creek banks had disappeared,
    and banks then were below my waist
As I walked from that long ravine
    into the calm below the bluff.

The calm in my mind ended when the car behind me honked.
The stalled traffic was moving again. I shifted into third gear. My life
was in "the rush" again.

# The Pillars

## ROBERT HARTLE

I hear the voices of a time gone by
In the ancient streets of Phillipii.
Towering pillars, silent and bold,
If they could speak, would tell stories of old

Of treachery, misery, mystery, and love,
That could lift your spirit as on wings of a dove,
People preaching of a god unseen,
Saying "Love your neighbor and don't be mean."

The ancient pillars stood so sublime,
Standing through everything but the test of time.
Two millennia have gone by
Since the pillars once reached for the sky.

The pillars now lie broken all around,
While some are scattered, others are in a mound.
The pillars are a testament of a people gone by
In the ancient streets of Phillipii.

PATRICIA LAWTON

# Money Can't Buy Everything
## (Or at Least It Shouldn't)

W hen I was young (a long time ago), we moved into a housing project. This was a new housing project built to accommodate the families with many children. On the other side of the street was a housing project called Pleasant Valley, also built for the American dream — two point five children.

I started walking on the other side of the street, wishing that someday I could afford one of those homes. I could not help but notice the difference. On our side we had one garbage can; they had two, complete with carrier to wheel them to the street. Of course with all our children, we needed two also, but we got by. The children got on top of the garbage and tramped it down.

The curtains for us: sheets did the trick until we could afford curtains; they, of course, had custom designed ones put up immediately. Their yards were landscaped right away; my son consumed half of ours before we could afford grass seed. Our cars remained outside because the garage was used to store all the children's bikes and toys; their car was neatly tucked in for the night.

I'm sure there were many other differences, but I was not privy to the inside of their homes during my walks. I continued my walks through their park-like neighborhood for many years with my children as they grew, and then with my grandchildren.

Eventually I walked through Pleasant Valley by myself after my family had all left home.

I always enjoyed the evenings — the flowers and the freshly mowed lawns and fresh bark. I mean fresh bark every year. I still longed to own one of the homes across the street with its fresh bark.

One evening as I started my walk, I noticed a strange glow

emanating from their neighborhood. It was an eerie blue color. A sound permeated the air — a humming sound, a buzzing sound, and a sizzling sound. It was all around me. There was no reprieve from it. It came from every home. I walked to the end where a creek bubbles through, but I could still hear it. I had to come back, so I took the road that paralleled the first, but I could not escape the sound.

All the Pleasant Valley neighbors owned one. What was this newest thing? A bug zapper, of course. I hurried back to my own neighborhood, grateful at last that we could not afford something. Gosh, it was peaceful there.

NANCY COVERT

# Treetop House

The young woman glanced from the highway to the crumpled sheet of handwritten directions that had been her Beatrice* during the past two and a half hours. She spotted the stoplight where she'd been told to turn.

"From the highway, proceed two blocks to the left, onto Church Street." She re-read the office manager's handwritten instructions. "The apartment is located at 210 Church Street, in a brown and yellow frame house next to the old Congregational Church."

Her destination was a small town — population 1200 — "in the heart of God's Country," she'd been told. News about finding room in an old manse had convinced her parents that, even though it wasn't what they'd hoped — it would be suitable for their first-born chick. What better place to begin a new life, she'd laughed when the office manager told her about the place. If it wasn't just right, she promised she'd look for other accommodations. In the meantime, she was eager to settle in and begin her career.

The back seat and trunk of her elderly brown/beige sedan was stacked to window level with an antique portable typewriter, suitcases and an assortment of discarded grocery store boxes. All her earthly possessions — except for those still in storage — were crammed into a dozen square feet. The landlady waved a welcome.

"It's not the destination, it's the journey." She'd read those words somewhere in the past year, and that trite truism had burrowed itself into a convoluted nook of her mind — an organ whose capacity would be crammed even further in coming weeks and beyond.

Her eastbound trip to the isolated border community wasn't the one her parents had hoped she'd make. They'd assumed she would at

*Beatrice: Dante's legendary guide

least temporarily revisit her first nest after graduating. This leg of the journey, though, was only 300 miles to the east, not 3,000.

Like Indiana Jones' "Last Crusade" she'd taken a brave leap of faith into the unknown. She hoped it would not be her last, but only the beginning. The leap came after one of the dozens of resumés she'd sent off had landed at the top of the heap in some managing editor's wire in-basket, in some remote town in a neighboring state. He'd liked what he saw, invited her for an interview and hired her "on the spot" for a journalist's job on one of the newspaper's even-more-remote satellite publications. Not exactly Nellie Bly — but even she had to start somewhere.

That had been two weeks earlier. Much of what had happened in the interim had faded into the background as she dismantled the familiar collegiate safety net she'd strung four years earlier.

She signed the lease and added the key to the chained collection, then followed the plump middle-aged woman up the creaky stairs to the second floor for an official look-see. In a burst of domesticity, she made half a dozen round trips to transfer the car's contents to her new quarters. This was followed by an initial effort to imprint her style on her new digs. An hour later, she poured a glass of iced tea (a full pitcher stored in the miniscule refrigerator, compliments of the management) and kicked back in the lumpy armchair to take stock.

The upper floor of what was once home to a large family had been subdivided into two small apartments. Apartment A was at the top of the stairs. To the left was a narrow alcove that sheltered a postage-stamp-sized kitchen. Beneath a small screened window draped with a faded pair of yellow gingham curtains, stood two rickety wooden chairs and an equally rickety small wood table. Straight ahead were a dark brown coffee table, a pair of mismatched plaid chairs, a reading lamp and a couch. Along the right wall was a Mission-style library table. A few feet farther, a narrow hallway led to the bedroom and bath. Not the Ritz, but the price was right.

Draining her glass, she headed toward the bedroom, unpacked and hung her clothes in the small, curtain-covered closet to the left of the bed. She unwrapped a brand new pair of flamboyantly printed sheets and added the faded Dresden Plate quilt her great-grand-mother had pieced as the final touch. A bouquet of radiant King Alfred daffodils in a green hobnail glass jar had been placed in the center of the well-worn four-drawer, pine-veneered dresser where the new tenant's towels, linens and "unmentionables" were now stored.

An errant spring breeze redolent of spring blossoms drifted through the window, refreshing the air with its scent. Returning to the living room — "sitting room" sounded more literary — she stopped to savor her living quarters, pour another glass of iced tea, and open her journal.

She began to write.

*Looking through the kitchen window I notice that the Manse — like something out of a Jane Austen novel — is surrounded by a grove of alder, maple, lilac, and apple — the swelling buds a silent tribute this commencement.*

*Verdant late afternoon light filters through translucent stained-glass-like leaves, creating a living-in-a-tree-house sensation, minus the downside of arachnid (yech!) intrusions or other creepy crawlies; a flock of robins and song sparrows perch on choir stall branches, chirping a greeting.*

*The entryway table lamp is an unusual shape — there's something familiar about its design — obviously a recycled something, but what? That is the question. Half a dozen green webs flare out from a center post, drilled to house the wiring and light fixture. A fan-pleated cream-colored shade tops the lamp like a lady's tea party hat, appropriate because this is a festive moment. I better understand Woolf's passionate desire for a room of her own.*

For a few moments longer, the domestic mystery's solution lay just beyond her grasp until the mental wheels ground to a halt. Then the ah-ha revelation came as the latter-day Sherlock solved the puzzle. This once-upon-a-time washing machine agitator, now reincarnated as a lamp, was definitely a conversation piece — the perfect accessory for her tree top home, and with a nod to Wordsworth — sensations sweet for future thought.

# Grave Dreams
## DAVID SWEET

How do you dream?
Do the cobwebs of your life
Suck you in and hold your mind?

Like an ax falling,
Your blissful childhood dreams
Cease and you're suddenly in a
Desperate place of no choice:
A pitch blackness with no sound,
A space that becomes smaller and smaller
As you fall through it.
Your being can't help;
There is no fight;
Your very soul is compressed in its vise.
Your breath is squeezed
Until you awaken with a start,
Blood chilling adrenaline
Coursing through your body like fire.
The breath finally comes back
But the fear and shock stay
And stay and stay…

Your life continues
But you never know when it will appear
To let you know your mind
Is still well within its grasp.
Your soul copes as well:
Here and there a puddle of
Black water with no reflection,
Your normal world.

Years pass and you search back,
"A simple digging up" of those
Old memories — or so you think —
Only to discover the dreams were exactly
What was happening in your life at that time.

So you excavate the coffin
Shovel by shoveful until there it is:

> *How dare you open me?*
> *We are the adults.*
> *We know what's best for you!*

Now it is your choice:
Open slowly or pry quickly.
A large burst forth
Or a final steady release.

There! It is done!
The unburial.
The pit.
The coffin.

Turn to the blue sky,
The towering maple looking down,
The birds on the wing,
The harmony of Nature alive.
A warm breeze gently surrounds
And welcomes you as a part,
Welcomes all of you....
Welcome back.

PATRICIA LAWTON

# The Sugar Spoon

Why it ever became a sugar spoon is still a mystery to me. I mean sugar bowls are attractive, but this spoon was tarnished and plain, except for an asterisk at the tip. And so thin it looked battered and bent. It first appeared in the family in 1932. That was when my Aunt Edith, in the eighth grade at the time, found it in her lunch pail instead of the nice silver spoon she had taken to school.

My mother, who was her older sister, decided she liked it and took it, according to my aunt. I became aware of its existence about 1949 when I was four years old. We used to leave our doors unbolted in those days. Once when we were not at home, my Uncle Bill came by with a friend, made some coffee, and swiped the spoon. I should also mention that he drew ants all over the calendar in the kitchen, but that is another story. He and Doug, his friend, were heading off to parts unknown and took the spoon with them. When they reached their destination — I think it was somewhere in Mexico — the spoon was returned to us, packed in a toothpaste box. That became the mode of transportation over the next 30 years.

Since that time the spoon has traveled to Texas, California, and Arizona for the winter. As family members became involved, we children became co-conspirators — giving it to them when my mom wasn't looking. Once my Uncle Bill, who started the whole thing, broke the spoon in half. Well, he searched a long time until he found one that resembled it. But the replacement was thicker. Needless to say, my mom either called or wrote so convincingly that back came the original spoon, soldered back together in the middle. We don't know what happened to the imposter spoon.

The original spoon went with us to Germany where it stayed for two years in our sugar bowl. When we returned to the States, the spoon started its travels again. Even though my mother could no longer get about, the sugar spoon continued its journeys. In time it went skydiving in Alaska, to Singapore with the Merchant Marine, proudly to the Rose Bowl, and many more places that have been lost to memory.

Eventually my mother started to worry that the spoon would be lost. My brother decided to make a plaque of all the places it had been. Then he sprayed the spoon gold.

The sugar spoon ended back in the silverware drawer where it languished for years. I used to feel sad when I saw it, remembering all the fun. But maybe its time has passed. The sugar bowl now contains tiny blue and pink packets.

SHANNON O'DONNELL

# Blood and Roses

William Francis Harkins was a veteran of the War Between the States. His grandson Tom remembered the old man dressed in Union Blue on the Fourth of July, listening to the speeches with dry eyes. His half-empty sleeve was a story untold. When Tom asked where the old man had fought or why he'd come to farm out West, far from his home place, William Francis only shook his head and waved off the questions with his one hand.

His wife, Lydia Stillwater, was born and raised in Pennsylvania. She was a square woman in her youth, with a slightly flattened nose and dark brown hair. Union soldiers used her family farm as a hospital after the battle at Gettysburg. They'd stayed only a week, but Lydia remembered the blood. The dining room was used for amputations. The blood soaked into the polished wooden floors. The doctors worked so fast there was no time to dispose of shattered arms and legs, so they pitched them out the window into her mother's rose bushes. When Lydia tried to save the roses, her mother held her back. "They're strong, Lyddie, let them be. They'll have their day again." The roses disappeared under the carnage.

When the army left, Lydia and her parents buried the bits and pieces of the soldiers and tried to clean the mess. The floors never gave up their rusty stains. The roses never recovered. The farm smelled of death. They abandoned it in 1868 and moved to town. She was twenty-eight by then, a woman made solemn by war and its aftermath. Two years later, she met William Francis.

Many war veterans were in the streets. William Francis was just one more the day she met him. His half arm wasn't the only feature she noted. She recognized his war weariness, but noticed it slipped away when he sang. She taught him new songs and by the time he'd learned a dozen, she was in love with him. He claimed it was at her very own farm that he'd lost his arm, that he'd seen the doctor toss it out the window with barely a glance. He didn't mention the roses and Lydia indulged him. Hers wasn't the only farm taken over to serve as a hospital during those grim days. He may have been nearby and that was enough. Fate had done the rest.

She was the one who called him William Francis. He'd been "Billy Frank" when he was growing up and in the Army. But he'd been through war and he'd lost his arm. She thought that deserved some recognition. When they married, the preacher asked if she would take William Francis as her husband. From that day on, he was William Francis to her.

Lydia was the one who suggested the move west soon after their marriage. "Too many people suffering and scrabbling here," she said. "We need a new place." So they'd come west through the Dakotas and into Montana. She'd liked Montana with its wide grassy plains and the sky unbounded by hills.

But William Francis shook his head. "Too many people back east. Not enough people here. We have to have some folks nearby." They moved on, over the Rockies into Idaho and then to the Washington Territory. They tried several places until they found this spot with wild prairies and a strong river. Others made the trip with them and those who finally stopped set up tents nearby and spent the spring making plans and marking out the land.

In time Lydia and William Francis had eight children, five who lived. Two girls died in infancy and a falling tree killed a gangly nine-year-old boy. Their three-room house lasted them a few years, and they added two more rooms over time. Each Christmas the boys ran in circles through the house and made every doorway an escape into safety. Wood fires made the whole house warm, the pungent smell of freshly peeled oranges spiced the air, and the clatter of kettle and spoon promised good things in the making.

When his grandson Tom was twelve, William Francis told him of the afternoon he'd faced down a bear in a newly cleared bit of woods. "I jumped on a stump, y'see," and he demonstrated how he'd used his half-arm to steady the rifle while he cocked it. The bear made three circles around him, coming in closer and baring its teeth. Then the old man pointed to a spot just beyond Tom and said, "Ka-bang! And there he went, howling into the woods. Never came back either. I went looking for him for weeks, thinking he'd make good

126

meals for the winter, but he was long gone." Then he laughed. "I don't figure he ever tried to go up against a man with one arm again. Maybe he learned his lesson."

Tom spent part of that summer trying to copy his grandfather's feat. Maybe because he was only twelve, he told himself, or maybe because he hadn't a soldier's training, he couldn't do it. He didn't love the old man any less.

William Francis lived another eleven years after that summer. In time, Tom came to live in the old house, himself an old man. He was gray and gaunt as the forgotten scarecrow in his last five acres. He hadn't planted anything for years. He stared at the field in the morning, certain he should know it, or at least know what it was for, but his mid-morning coffee chased away the certainty.

Only the roses flourished and they grew whether or not he paid attention to them. Their bright blooms spoke of other places, other lifetimes. William Francis had planted them not long after the house was built. He called one "Lyddie" but never told her which one. After she died at age sixty, William Francis cut a wheelbarrow full of blooms and took them to her grave. Every summer and every fall until he died, he covered her with a blanket of fragrance and color.

# Coming Home
## PATRICIA LAWTON

Leave not my remains
    to weep in this forsaken land.
Sent forever too late
    to extricate
    the enemy dug deep in the ground.

No Flanders Field awaits me here
    like my father's war far away.
The jungle creeps
    to where I sleep
    and soon I shall be no more.

# Dream Makers

SHERRY BENIC

We are the dreamers, the weavers and spinners,
Singers in a minor key.
The smoke and the mirrors
Hide in our minds:
We twist them and bend what you see.

We give you nightmares and daydreams,
Giggles and fears,
Braided and woven together
Into a crazy old quilt to hide your head under
While we shape the wind and the weather.

And the moon trills its tale
While Hecate spins
Threads invisible and free;
Gossamer strands entwine you and bind you,
We control what you think and can see.

Yes...
We are the dreamers, the weavers and spinners,
And our siren cry beckons
Through the mists of a scheme,
Enrapturing, capturing,
Bewitching, beguiling,
Luring you into a dream.

# Dreamy

(Romance and Adventure)

*Speak low, if you speak love.*
*—Shakespeare*

# Desire

### P. June Diehl

Delicate snowflakes
Drifting
Down

Dangling
Dancing
Delighting to the ground.

Display of cold
Daring to grow old
Days are but microseconds of time.

Danger?
Destroyed?
Death be found?

Dare to believe,
Decree the delightful forms,
Death not be found!

Destroyed not ñ only transformed,
Decries the delightful forms,
Danger nowhere is found.

Desire,
Design of one to be
Dreams of being part of the many.

# Dan Sloan

# Quiet Island

I need to find that island once more. It's been three years since I last left it, and I need to go back. I am searching for Quiet Island. I found it once when I was hiking at Mowich Lake on Mount Rainier. My wife had just died and I was thinking of joining her. The day fit my outlook. It was cold and damp. The fog layer was thick but bright. The sun would eventually burn off the layer of low clouds.

While walking along the path next to the lake thinking back on happier days, I grew sadder the longer I continued. What was my life going to be like alone without Jan, my lifelong companion? We had been married for thirty-two years. Many of the years were happy; some of the years were sad; a few of the years were severely trying. I first saw Quiet Island shortly after I met my future wife.

As a sophomore in college, I had been dating Jan's roommate, Karen. She was sort of a wild girl. Actually, she was engaged, but she refused to be stifled by that arrangement. Karen figured that what her fiancée didn't know would be just fine. I asked her to go with me to the homecoming dance. At first Karen accepted, then later that same week she called me and told me that her fiancée was coming to town for the weekend and she would be going to the dance with him. Her fiancée! For a few moments I was quite speechless. I started to get angry. If she was already engaged, what right did she have going out with other men? As the anger welled up inside me, Karen was going on about how her roommate had just broken up with her high school sweetheart. Her roommate was in a blue funk and needed to get out of the dorm room. Since I was such a nice guy, and already had tickets to the dance, would I please meet her roommate and ask her to go to the dance? She would make all the arrangements for us to get together at the Student Union Building for a Coke date the next afternoon. Jan would be with Karen at 3 o'clock. They would be sitting at the table where Karen and I usually met.

I finished my last class the next day and walked to the Student Union Building (SUB). I needed a Coke. The caffeine and sugar would give me the jolt I needed to carry me for the hour between now and when it would be time for me to go to work at the dining hall; I was a part-time dishwasher. My job would give me a reason to break off the date and bail out if I needed to. I entered the cafeteria area of the SUB and looked towards the table where I expected to find Karen. She was sitting with her back towards me.

Jan was sitting facing towards me, her back to the wall. Above her head was a bulletin board. There were floodlights lighting the board behind her, one of them directed to the spot directly behind her head. The circle of light gave Jan a halo. Jan was talking animatedly to Karen, and she didn't seem to be too happy with her friend. I found out later that Jan didn't really want to go to the SUB, but did so to prevent trouble between Karen and her fiancée.

Jan wasn't a beautiful girl, but I found her attractive. There was a familiarity about her that I could not place. I thought I had met her somewhere before, but knew that we had never met. I approached the table.

"Hi, Karen."

Karen gave a little jump. "Hi, Dan. You startled me. How do you keep sneaking up on me like that? That must be the tenth time you've done that to me."

Jan smiled a little and bumped a chair in my direction.

Karen said, "I'd like you to meet my roommate. Jan, this is Dan. Dan, this is Jan. She's a history ed major. Dan is an electrical engineering major."

As I sat down, Jan asked, "When did we meet? I think I know you from somewhere."

"No, I don't think we've ever met before. I need a Coke, can I get one for either of you?"

"Thanks, no, I have this glass of water," said Jan.

"Yes, I'd like a cherry Coke," said Karen.

I went through the cafeteria line and bought my Coke and Karen's cherry Coke. When I came back to the table we talked for a while before Karen excused herself to head off to her next class. Jan and I continued the conversation. Too soon it was time for me to head off to work. I made a date with Jan to meet again the next day. I usually have difficulty talking to people the first time I meet them, but Jan was easy to talk to. I was immediately as at ease with her as I ever was with any of my long time friends.

That night I had an unusual dream. That was the first time that I saw Quiet Island.

I dreamed I was walking along the shore of a beautiful mist-shrouded lake. The mists slowly parted, revealing a small island. Tall fir trees with their tops hidden by the fog created a gray-on-gray barrier in the background. Pine trees along the island shore stood out clearly. Along one side a stark white fallen log was half in and half out of the water. The water between the island and me was clear and shallow, the ripples on the surface seemingly moving from me towards the island, beckoning me. I waded in. The water felt shockingly cold; my shoes filled with ice. My feet recoiled and tried to climb out of my shoes. I pushed farther out. My calves felt the iciness and tried to knot up in protest. I forced my way through the protecting waters to the welcoming shore. I squished over to the log, sat down, removed my shoes and twisted the cold water out of my socks. After I put my shoes and socks back on, my feet started to warm themselves. That is when I saw an animal trail pushed through the obscuring underbrush. I followed the trail into a brightly-lighted clearing. The light came from all directions at once. I strode into the center of the clearing, and just stood there. I could hear some quiet murmuring like a gentle breeze in the treetops. Soon I could perceive individual sounds. The sounds became more clear and distinct.

"Ah, Daniel is here," said a smooth comforting baritone voice.

"Well, its about time. He should have come sooner. It's been nearly two years since his mother died. He was supposed to come then," said an alto voice.

"Well, he's here now. Welcome, Daniel," said the baritone.

"What did she mean, I should have been here sooner?" I asked.

"You are a special person for us, and we want to help. When your mother died, we tried to get through to you to help you through your anguish. You refused to listen then. You retreated into a tightly closed shell. You kept all of your emotions to yourself. Your soul went into suspended animation. You have existed on the physical plane only. We have been doing what we can to reach you, but it's just now that you have cracked your shell enough for us to make contact," soothed the mellow baritone.

The alto voice spoke, "You have just met a girl. She will be a great comfort to you if you will just open up and be yourself."

"You will also be able to help Janice in the course of your lives together. We will always be here for you. You will need us in the future. Keep your soul open to those around you. When the great turning points in your life occur, you will seek us out. We will be here waiting. Now, go back, take comfort in the knowledge that you are doing what you are destined to do."

The dream voices were right. Jan and I were married the next year. At every major turning point in my life I have had the same recurring dream. Quiet Island would appear in a dream. I would wade over to the island and talk to the same two voices about what I was doing, what my choices were, and what I had chosen to do. The voices would encourage me to go forth, do what I had decided on. I have had no regrets in following the path that I seem to have been predestined to follow.

After Jan died, I had a lot of trouble going to sleep, and once I finally fell asleep I had to fight with myself to get out of bed the next day. I would sleep till noon. Normally food was a passion; I love to cook, but food became optional. Work was out of the question. I couldn't carry a thought to any conclusion. I could not make decisions about anything. I sat and stared at the television set, not caring what was flickering in front of my non-seeing eyes. Nothing brought a smile to my face. Communicating with another person was nearly impossible.

I was drawn to Mount Rainier looming in the distance. I derived a strange comfort in just gazing on the mountain. Finally I went there. I drove up the backside through Wilkeson, following the signs directing me towards Mowich Lake. The paved road ran out, yet I continued into the enveloping cloud-engulfed trail. The road stopped at a camp grounds. I parked the car and started to walk the beckoning shoreline trail. I came to an isolated peninsula and sat on a log. I was lost in thought staring out into the mist that covered the lake. I could barely discern a lone fir tree in the fog bank. As I concentrated on the tree, the mists parted and there was Quiet Island. I waded over and sought the bright clearing.

"Welcome Daniel," said the familiar baritone. "We know how severely hurt you are. That is why we wanted you to come to us physically."

"Yes," said the alto. "We do not want you to suffer so. You will not cease to exist. You have many happy years ahead of you."

"Rejoice in the idea that Janice is no longer suffering from her illnesses as she had been for the last five years. You made her last five years worth living. If you had not been around, she would have been unable to be as independent or able to live the way she wanted to live," said the baritone.

"Just lie down here for a few moments," soothed the alto. "Relax, this crisis has passed."

I lay down in the warmth of the brightly-lit meadow. I felt a soothing hand gently brush my hair, and I fell asleep. When I awoke, I was sitting in the driver's seat of my car. My shoes and pants were dripping water onto the carpeting under my feet, and I was no longer in the depths of despair. I took comfort in the knowledge that Jan was no longer suffering. The mists of the day were gone. The sun was shining brightly. It was time for me to begin living again. I drove back down the mountain and into my future.

Now I have achieved the goals I set in my life with Jan. I have reached another major turning point in my life. I have prospered. I have enough money to retire, I have met another woman, and I am happy. I need to find Quiet Island again. This time I want to thank the two voices that kept me alive that day three years ago.

# Rocking Chair
## STEVE RUDIS

An old gold miner sat in his rocking chair
    on the porch of his log cabin,
    looking out over land
    he had worked for many years.
Slowly back and forth,
    slowly back and forth
    the chair did move,
Like the pendulum of a clock,
    ticking away the days.

DONNA ANDERSON

# Beginnings

*B*eginnings is a nice word. It conjures up happy thoughts and memories — a new day or a new start. For Sheila, it had a special meaning. She was pregnant. A new life. It would be a new beginning for her and for Ralph. Now all she had to do was tell him.

*He would say, "How was your day?"*

*And I could say, '"Oh just fine. I am pregnant."*

*Or I could say, '"Darling, there is something I want to tell you."*

*Or I could say, '"Here's a surprise for you, I am going to have a baby."*

*Or I could just wait and tell him later.*

Ralph was having an interesting day too. The boss had just told him they were moving his part of the company's operation to Chicago, and Ralph would have a promotion, more money and moving expenses, if he would move with them. Yes he could move most of his staff with him. He would have until tomorrow to make the decision. He already knew he would take the job. Becoming Head of the Division was another step in the direction he wanted. And more money? Of course he wanted that, Now all he had to do was tell Sheila.

That night conversation was stilted and practically non-existent. They both had busy thoughts of their own.

Sheila thought Ralph was just tired and grouchy, as he often was. When she asked what was wrong, why he was so quiet, he snapped at her and said it was "just work." Well, she was right to wait and tell him another night, when he was happier.

Ralph wanted to talk about the move, but Sheila was so scatter-brained that night. She couldn't even keep her mind on fixing dinner and it was burned, so he decided to wait until she could concentrate better. *She's usually sort of a featherbrain and flighty, but it's worse tonight.*

Sheila was a "hair designer," a title her salon used to indicate that she cut hair. It also allowed them to charge outrageous prices for her services, and she was always booked fully. She thought this was a good job for her now. After the baby came she could stay home if Ralph wanted her to, or take the baby to the day care next door to the shop while she worked. She thought he would be pleased that she had planned ahead.

Ralph gave the boss his answer early the next morning. The only questions they had was how soon could Ralph make the move and could Ralph fly to Chicago the next day to spend a few days going over this move in detailed meetings? He was more excited now. A new job, new town, a new beginning.

When Sheila came home, she found Ralph packing. A trip to Chicago. That wasn't so unusual, but it was so sudden. *Oh, so what?* she thought. *I'll tell him when he gets back.* Good thing she had stopped by the cleaners today.

Sheila had been feeling light-headed and nauseated all day. This pregnant thing was starting out not to be fun, Or maybe it was just the flu. Of course, that's what it was. She didn't feel like cooking dinner, but Ralph said he had had a big lunch, and a sandwich in front of the TV was okay with him. She took a warm bath and went to bed. She was asleep when he got there.

The Chicago trip was as good as Ralph thought it would be. He was shown his new corner office and he was wined and dined like a celebrity. He knew everyone in the office already, but now there was a new respect in their voices and demeanor. Yes, this would be a great new beginning. He flew home full of plans and happy thoughts, happy until he thought of telling Sheila. How would she take the news? He decided he would take her out to lunch the next day. It would be just the two of them in a nice quiet place. Then he could tell her the exciting news.

While he was in Chicago, Sheila decided to see a doctor. She still had the nausea. Was this normal? He told her yes, this was pretty normal, especially with first babies. He confirmed that she was definitely pregnant and told her when to come back. He said to call him if the nausea persisted. Now she knew she needed to tell Ralph right away so he would understand why she was out of sorts.

Ralph went directly to the office from the plane. He called

Sheila to make arrangements for lunch. She arranged her day too. She was so happy. This would be a perfect place to tell him.

Sheila was already seated when he arrived. He didn't kiss her hello. She thought this was odd, but he must have something on his mind. She was bursting with the news.

"Ralph, I have something to tell you…," she started, but he cut her off.

"I have something to tell you too. Let me go first." He started by reminding her about how hard he worked, and she agreed. He had worked long days and many weekends. She agreed again. He was trying to get ahead in his company and now it had happened. He was receiving a promotion that would necessitate his move to Chicago. He had loved his time here and cherished his time with her, but now it was over. He went on to remind her that when they moved in together they had shared expenses, but since he was the one moving out, he would pay the whole rent and utilities for the apartment until the end of the lease in August — his way of being fair. Since there was nothing to keep him here, he would be moving this weekend. He would pack what he needed this afternoon and be gone before she got home. He'd send for the rest of his stuff if she would just put it into some boxes. It had been nice living with her, and he wished her a very happy life. And hey, maybe they would run into each other in the future.

Sheila just sat there. Now she would never be able to tell him her news. Now this beginning was hers alone. All hers.

# Passions Awakened

Janice R. Carlsen

Passions awakened,
No longer are meek;
Never mistaken
As lacking or weak.

Consuming desire,
Enraptured in joy,
Quivering afire,
Sensitive and coy.

Tender endearments,
Lovingly spoken,
Truly in essence,
Offered in token.

Tears on my pillow
No longer are found;
Strong as the willow,
My love is abound.

Ecstasy carnal,
A true endeavor;
My love eternal,
I pledge forever.

JEAN C. HANNAN

# Night Watch

S andy slowed his woodsman's stride at the edge of the forest and stopped to take stock of his appearance. The heavy mackinaw was tidy and as much a part of Sandy as the graying reddish hair that projected from under his plaid cap. The mittens, which he removed from his strong but well-shaped hands, matched the stockings that showed a deep green at the top of his boots. He bent forward, and with one hand picked burrs from the stocking tops and cleaned the mud from his boots. With his other hand he gently stroked his dog, Scot.

"Stay, boy," Sandy told the dog. Then, mustering all of his courage, Sandy drew himself up straight, entered the pathway, walked to the cabin in the clearing and knocked on the door.

The door did not open at once. Sandy's mind bristled with questions: Have I knocked on the wrong door? Is there another cabin within miles? Why did I tell those folks I would come up here? I don't know anything about women — still don't after all these years. Sandy was about to knock again when, with a slight swoosh, the door jamb released the heavy planked door.

"Yes?" the woman asked.

Sandy could not see her. "It's MacLaren...come to sit with you...until they come for..."

"How kind," the woman answered, opening the door wide enough for Sandy to enter. She turned toward the coffin resting there in the room as if to explain her quiet tone, her reluctance to open the door. Then she turned back to Sandy, her slight body still. At the same time she motioned to him to remove his mackinaw, cap and mittens, indicating wordlessly that the fire would warm him.

141

Even the fire burned noiselessly as Sandy's wraps were hung on a nail by the door.

"We're all painfully sorry about your husband, Ma'am," Sandy began, speaking for neighbors of the wilderness in the rote fashion used with the bereaved. "You must try to rest now. I'll sit here by the fire."

But the woman lowered herself slowly into a chair across from Sandy and looked into the fire, as if searching for consolation or answers. She threaded her fingers together in her lap and shook her head ever so slowly in quiet mourning.

Sandy could observe her now, this woman with her plainly knotted graying hair, her lined but beautiful face masked by sorrow. Her shawl was drawn into a loose knot across her breast, the only gesture toward the extra warmth and comfort she needed. Sandy tried to recall where he had seen her before. Oh, years ago, when we used to have dances, he thought; surely that was where I saw her. Yes, remember, Sandy old man, how she laughed as she danced? But she must have spent all life's laughs in tending her mountain man... and now he's gone. Will her gentle, sad face ever laugh again?

"Ma'am," Sandy urged again. "I'll be here ...try to get some rest."

This time she rose and, barely nodding her thanks, she stepped into the curtained-off corner of the cabin. Sandy looked into the fire for comfort. Without knowing why, he turned his thoughts back down the mountain and across the plains to his home in Indiana. A feeling of guilt tugged at him as he thought about that other world — the world where his father had been a botany professor at the university and had expected him, Malcolm, to succeed him.

But, Sandy reasoned now, it was just not to be. I would have been rooted to plants of one small frontier, when the whole West was filled with growing things of endless variety, and there was adventure as well.

"Malcolm," he could hear his mother's constant plea, "find some nice girl and settle down. That nice Ellen..." Sandy squirmed in his chair by the fire at the thought of nice Ellen. How long ago was that? I was never able to talk to women. Collecting plant specimens for the university, now that's something I could do, and I've done thousands.

Some men find women in this wilderness, though, Sandy mused. This old chap lying there dead — he found his woman. And now he's gone and she's lying there in grief. What's the sense of that? What's she going to do now? When the folks come to bury her man tomorrow she won't have anything but this cabin. I wonder where she came from? Can she go back home? No, I don't think so. Sandy shook himself more awake. She can't go home, any more than I can. The wilderness reaches out and claims us.

The hours crept on. The woman stirred behind the curtain. Sleep on, Sandy told her inaudibly. Sleep on — the night will go faster that way.

But her sleep was broken. She appeared, silently, and resumed the watch in her chair by the fire. As they sat looking into the fire, they broke their silence and spoke gently of the plan for neighbors to come to bury her husband.

"Will you stay on here?" Sandy asked.

Her hands gestured her indecision. "If I were young I would go back," she said, almost to herself. Sandy wanted to ask where that would be, but hesitated. She glanced at Sandy, self-consciously, and resumed her communion with the fire.

Then, startled, they both were roused to sounds from across the clearing. Sandy's ears picked up Scot's low woof that blended easily with voices. The neighbors were coming up the mountain, nearing the path in the clearing. The sounds brought Sandy and the woman to the awareness of dawn.

The night watch was over. Sandy had fulfilled his mission. He would be going now.

The woman extended her hand to show her appreciation. "What did you say your name is? I wasn't thinking very well when you came…"

"MacLaren," Sandy told her, "Sandy, they call me here in the mountains. I study plants — it's been my life work."

Sandy turned toward the door and reached for his mackinaw. The woman lifted her head and tentatively reached toward him. "Tell me, she asked, "are you called Malcolm?"

Sandy froze, then flushed. "Not here, I'm not. Why? Why do you ask?"

The woman cast a last, longing glance at her husband's coffin. With a pleading, anguished look she sighed, "I knew your Mother, Malcolm. I'm…I'm…Ellen."

# Nothing Is Impossible

## PETER JENNINGS

I don't know what to do
Except for the things
I'll do for you.

The thought of your touch
Runs shivers down my spine.
I love the way you kiss
When your lips touch mine.

A simple vision of your face,
Brings my spirit
Infinite grace.

The total love in your eyes,
Could make the
Devil rise.

Your long blonde hair
Is more radiant
Compared to the world
Out there.

The curve of your lips
I want to kiss even
Though implausible.

You made me realize,
Nothing is impossible.

Now, I don't know what to do,
But I know I'm in love with you.

JANELLE MERAZ HOOPER

# Free Pecan Pie

When she got back from her tennis game and showered, Maggie-Lynn didn't bother to put on makeup. Why bother? Her husband was out of town. It pained her to admit — even to herself — that it probably wouldn't have mattered anyway. It was getting harder and harder to dazzle that man.

Years ago, he would have wanted her with or without mascara. Now he looked for reasons to put her off. Why? she wondered. She was big-boned, but she watched her weight, so her shape was still good. Sure, her luggage had shifted a little here and there, but so what? He didn't look the same as he did in college, either.

She turned from the mirror and padded barefooted down the hallway to the kitchen in search of a piece of pecan pie. Every refrigerator in Mississippi had pecan pie in it. It was a rule of some kind. As she rummaged through shelf after shelf of leftover snacks from a party they'd had the night before, her mind flipped through the file on her thirty-year marriage.

Okay, so things hadn't been real great between her and Roger lately. But they'd had trouble before and weathered it. She was so sure that things would change again for the better that she'd raced through a local lingerie store that afternoon and bought a very expensive sleep set from a Philippine designer who specialized in cutout lace.

This latest shopping spree was inspired by a phone call from a friend the day before, who called to tell her that she saw Roger leaving a jewelry store with a small package. Sue-Anne hadn't needed X-ray vision to know it was a bracelet box. A survivor of three marriages, she could identify all six shapes of jewelry boxes at a glance. From this particular store, a box with a silk magnolia was top of the line. The storm, whatever it was, must have passed.

Maggie-Lynn had given up on finding any leftover pie and was slicing frozen cantaloupe stuffed with vanilla ice cream onto a plate when the phone rang. She answered with a lilt in her voice. Maybe it was Roger.

"Hell-lo-o!"

"Maggie? I've got bad news, Hon." It was Cindy, her sister, who worked as Roger's secretary. "You know that bracelet that Roger brought back to the office? It's gone. He took it with him to Louisiana."

Maggie-Lynn missed the kitchen stool and crumpled onto the floor. "I wonder what kind of bracelet it was," she said weakly through her tears.

"If you really want to know, we have a way to find out. He took it to the company insurance department to have it appraised. I'm sure that Beverly scanned it into a file. She's working late tonight. Want me to call her?"

"Yes. Ask her to wait for me. I can be there in twenty minutes. I want to see for myself."

"Okay. I'll meet you in my office."

Beverly pulled up the bracelet photo on her computer and the three sat around the monitor and looked at it like it was a cadaver and they were coroners. In a way, it was a cadaver — of a dead marriage.

"It's valued at twelve hundred dollars," Beverly said as she read the report.

"It's small," Cindy said. "And dainty."

"Who can she be?" Maggie-Lynn wanted to know.

"By the looks of the bracelet, someone very young, feminine and small," Beverly offered.

"Who do we know like that?" Maggie-Lynn asked her sister.

"I have an idea," Cindy said hesitantly. "There was a salesperson in our office last week. She started coming around when I was on vacation. Her name is Roxanne."

"What was she selling?"

"GPS jewelry. She was from some company in Canada. They have a whole line of jewelry that has those global positioning systems built into them. I saw some of them. Watches, bracelets, and pins — that sort of stuff. They're expensive and look like normal pieces of jewelry. It could be her. I know he put in a big order."

146

"Look at the charms," Maggie-Lynn said. "A tiny palm tree, a yacht, and a martini glass. All with tiny diamonds. Maggie-Lynn gasped when Beverly scrolled down and she saw the last charm, a diamond ring. "Oh, God. I don't believe it. He's going to leave me! Where is he staying, Sis?" Maggie-Lynn hurriedly picked up her purse and keys.

"At the Plantation Inn on the outskirts of New Orleans. You're not driving over there?"

"I am. I have to see this for myself."

Maggie-Lynn raced home and packed a big purse with a clean change of clothes and took off for the Mississippi-Louisiana border. Her cell phone rang before she crossed the Louisiana state line.

"Maggie? Where are you?" Cindy asked.

"Close to the state line. Why?"

"Turn around. Now! Do it, Sis. Then call me back."

Cindy's sense of urgency alarmed Maggie-Lynn. She made a quick turn into a rest stop.

What's going on?" Maggie-Lynn asked her sister over her cell phone.

"I had an idea and went back to the office to check it out."

"What?"

"Roger bought a watch for himself from her and she brought it in yesterday. In the package was a freebie—a GPS device that sticks on a car. I checked, and it's gone."

"You don't think…?"

"I do. How handy is that? The little trollop comes with her own protection system. Look for something on your car that doesn't look like it belongs there. It's small."

"First, I'm going to drive back to the junction. That way they won't know which direction I was headed."

Maggie-Lynn raced her Jaguar to the outlet mall near the state line. It was a believable destination. After she parked in a well-lighted area, she walked around the exterior of her car until she spotted a small medallion, smaller than a dime, on her license plate frame. "Bingo!" she told her sister. "Do you think they caught me?"

"Maybe. They'll think you missed the turn-off and doubled back — if they were even checking it. They may have been in the restaurant. What are you going to do now?"

"Continue on," Maggie-Lynn said. "But first I need you to come pick up this whatever it is and take it back to my driveway."

"Okay. I could stand a little shopping therapy anyway. See you in thirty minutes."

"Look for me right in front of the shoe store."

While she waited for her sister, Maggie-Lynn had some time to think. A palm tree, a yacht, a diamond ring. The bracelet was full of clues. Roger must have met her when he went to Hawaii to work on that condominium project. It all started then, in Hawaii — a place Roger always claimed he hated. Well, Roger, now I hate it too.

When Roger and Roxanne went down for dinner, she took her laptop with her. She said it was a present. "You're giving me a laptop?" Roger asked as he glanced at the top of the unit emblazoned with her company's logo. "You'll see." Roxanne patted the computer smugly.

The diamond charm bracelet was inside Roger's breast pocket, and he gave it to Roxanne the minute their mint juleps arrived. While he fastened it around her wrist, his eyes darted about the room.

"Roger, are you nervous?"

"It's the first time we've been together so close to home."

"I thought so. I have the same problem when I'm in Vancouver. I'm always looking for my husband, eh?"

"You're married?"

"Of course. Who do you think watches Alex when I travel?"

"Who's Alex?"

"My nine-month-old."

"You never mentioned a husband and child." Roger sat back and looked at the woman he thought he knew and saw a total stranger.

"They're hardly part of the company sales pitch." As she talked, she tapped the keyboard. "Uh-oh. We have a problem. I hoped to show you that Maggie was home."

"What?"

"I had an associate put a GPS — actually your freebie — on the back bumper of her car."

"You bugged my wife's car?"

"Yeah. She must have found it. The car isn't moving, but she is."

"What do you mean?" Roger stammered.

"The key chain I gave you to give her also has a GPS device in it."

"You bugged her twice? Where is she?"

"Do you know how I said when we first met that I'd like to meet your wife?" Roxanne drew a deep breath. "I'm about to get my wish.

148

She's coming in the door right now."

Roger turned to face his wife, who was moving determinedly between the tables toward them.

Maggie-Lynn couldn't manage a smile when she sat down, but she did manage to keep her voice low and purposeful. Roger started several times to say something, but his open mouth remained silent.

"Roger, we'll talk later. No forget that," she waved her hand as if to cancel the statement. "There's nothing to talk about, is there?" Turning to Roxanne, she said, "Nice bracelet, Roxanne. Is it new?" Then, with as much grace as she could muster, Maggie rose and left the table. After all, this was the South, she told herself. A lady wouldn't do something so unseemly as to make a scene. As she walked away, she could hear the two bickering behind her.

"You can cancel that order of watches for my executives," Roger snapped.

"I'm sorry, but company policy doesn't allow for the return of engraved pieces. You had each watch initialed, eh?"

Still shaking, Maggie-Lynn was making her way to the concierge when she passed the front desk. The staff was loading a cart with little Styrofoam boxes of pecan pie with plastic forks taped on top. There was one for each guest. Pecan pie was a tradition in New Orleans, like peanut butter ice cream in Alabama and pineapples in Hawaii. Maggie-Lynn stopped and smiled her sweetest smile. "I'm with Roger Heitt. We'll just take ours now. We're going to look at the river."

The staff nodded and crossed two names off their list. Maggie set the boxes securely at the bottom of her tote bag. When she reached the concierge, she gave him her valet ticket and a healthy tip and was rewarded with another free piece of pecan pie.

Down the road, a sign with a big blinking neon alligator had a reader board that caught Maggie-Lynn's eye: it offered free pecan pie with a car wash. Maggie-Lynn pulled in. While her car was being pulled through the soapy brushes, she removed the fork off the top and ate all of the latest piece of pie. It gave her a real sugar high, but it wasn't enough to erase the fatigue she felt.

That's when she spotted one of her favorite hotel chains, The Cajun Court, flashing a sign with a dancing alligator wearing a top hat and tails and offering free pecan pie to its guests. Maggie-Lynn pulled in and signed the guest register. She put the new piece of pie at the bottom of her tote bag with the others before she dragged herself up to her room.

She needed to think. After years of watching her weight so she'd look good for Roger, a table full of pie — all of it hers — seemed awesomely excessive. She walked around the table and lightly ran her fingers over the little white box tops as she pondered her options. The way she saw it, at the moment she had two choices: she could eat the pie or not eat the pie. That was easy. She was going to eat the pie. Her marriage struck her as much the same: she could keep Roger...or not. That was easy too. She'd call her attorney in the morning.

Maggie stepped out on the balcony and took a deep breath of heavy Cajun air laced with honeysuckle. She wanted to cry. And she would. But first she'd call her sister to let her know she was okay — and have another piece of pecan pie.

CALUNA MITCHELL

# Yellowstone Angel

Two miles ahead were the cascading waters of the Yellowstone
River as they descended over a thousand feet into the
bottom of the golden canyon for which the river was named.
The thundering waters sang to me as I stood in awe of a sight that
adorned millions of post cards — all inadequate to articulate the
magnificence and the vital power of nature.

What a country to carry out my doctor's prescription for daily
walks. I had been waiting for this trail on the canyon rim to open.
Now on a perfect morning in late May, the chain and the "closed
sign" had vanished. Nothing lay between a childhood dream and
me. I walked on, experiencing the earth's vibrations from the weight
of the mighty river as it impacted the canyon's belly.

I had covered only a diminutive distance toward my goal when
the tremors intensified and a forceful roar behind me suppressed the
fall's song. I turned back to witness the scene that transformed my
spectacular dream into a surreal nightmare. Several feet of the path
behind me was sliding, almost silently, down the steep side of the
canyon past the steaming fumaroles at the river's edge and into the
deep icy raging waters.

Shaking, I headed down the remaining broad path, not absorb-
ing that what lay behind me might also be ahead of me. I turned the
bend. The trail was no longer wide. To continue on it, I would have
to press my body against the canyon wall and edge my way along the
rim that had been narrowed to a few inches as it left the main
canyon. I looked back the way I had come; the head of the trail was
not visible. The wall of the canyon rose ten to fifteen feet above me
at a steep angle, and there was no way to climb the crumbling earth.

I could forget about yelling for help; my voice was not going to be heard over the noise of the falls. It was too early for tourists, and the rangers wouldn't be concerned about me for another couple of hours. As the feeling of being trapped slowly crept into my being, I realized there was only one thing left besides reviewing my not-too-long life. I drew in a deep breath and looked up toward the bright azure sky. "Hi there! Boy, do I hope your request line is open, because I really need to ask for help again."

At that moment a small rock from overhead fell past me, followed by a few more of its friends; the ground began to rumble. Swallowing hard, I took a deep breath, and in an unsteady voice continued, "Got to go, I'll get back to you," and added, "I hope!"

I pressed my back against the warm canyon wall and advanced along the rim at a pace that resembled the slimy slugs of the Pacific Northwest. But it was fast enough; I stared as the ledge I had stood on only moments before also went down into the river below. I began to get dizzy, and silently affirmed, *Look up, not down; do not look down.*

So I looked across to the other side of the ravine, which was in the shadow cast by the not-so-friendly glare of the sun. I found a rock to focus on as I slowly worked my way forward.

Finally, I reached the shade, and I began to breathe deeply and greedily the thin mountain air. It dawned on me that I had been holding my breath during my journey along what remained of the trail. In the shade, the canyon wall was still frozen. I knew that when the shade disappeared, it was going to thaw out and become unstable, just like the opposite wall that was growing warmer as the sun climbed higher.

"Let's see. Where was I when I was interrupted? Oh yeah, I was going to ask you for some help. I got myself into this, but I don't think I can get myself out without help. The last few months have been pretty rough; you've been working double time to keep me alive. You and I have been through a lot. I can't see any sense in letting me slide into those steam vents to be boiled, poached, and spit out into an icy cold river then pulverized on the rocks. Could you figure out a way to rescue me, please? I'd really like that." Taking a deep breath, I concluded, "Better get moving while I can."

I walked out of one ravine to look into another. The trail became wider; I could get one foot in front of the other. Ahead of me part of the trail was missing. I could see that it had gone in the same direction as the trail behind me. I started to climb above the slide, trying to walk over that area. No such luck. The ground gave way under my feet and I had to leap for the ledge. I actually landed on my feet; I just didn't stay on them. I fell forward onto my hands. Once the ground stopped moving, except for the continuous tremors from the falls and my legs, I realized my hands were in indentations in the ground. I was a city-bred kid but I didn't have to be an expert tracker to recognize those tracks.

The ranger's lecture echoed in my head. "There is only one thing meaner than a hungry grizzly bear out of hibernation and that is a muh-ther hungry grizzly bear out of hibernation." I could see that my fingertips barely reached the toes of the paw prints beneath my hands. The deep gouges of the claws lay beyond my fingertips. Beside the tracks were paw prints smaller than my hands, miniature replicas of the larger prints.

"Some tourist guide you sent me," I sputtered.

I rose slowly with the expectation of hearing the roar of a mother bear. The falls and the eternal wind were the only sounds. "She outweighs me," I figured, "and where she can walk so can I." The bear and I have a long ways to go with no water, no food, or shade. It's getting pretty hot, and she's going to be even warmer dressed in fur. With my poor health, could I even make it? Those thoughts, those fears, I left unspoken.

The cub's tracks disappeared at that point. *She's carrying it.* I allowed time for the prints to fill with ground water and then followed. Around the next bend was a large boulder across the trail; the scratches on it indicated she had climbed it. I took a deep breath and clumsily scaled the huge rock, unable to see what was on the other side.

At the top, I was relieved to see more tracks, but no bears. There was a small pine tree decorated in golden blond grizzly fur. As I made my way past the tree, I tripped on one of its roots and the tree's branches carved up my leg as I slid by. I grabbed for whatever handhold or foothold I could find to keep me on the specter of a path. I knew I wasn't in danger of bleeding to death, but I didn't need the smell of the blood from my leg to encourage a thirsty and hungry grizzly.

I limped forward toward another boulder that lay under a ledge in the disappearing shade. It had strange white streaks on its side. It turned out to be crusted-over chunk ice. The bear had clawed out a large cavity of icy chunks. She had eaten her fill and left plenty for me.

I quenched my thirst and vainly tried to use the ice to slow the bleeding. Onward, following her tracks, I hobbled, looking toward the falls that didn't seem to be a whole lot closer. In and out of several ravines I followed the mother bear's tracks. The song of the falls slowly grew in volume, and presently dominated the air. The sun had risen higher and hotter; all the rocky walls radiated heat.

The energy gained from the ice was gone. I walk unsteadily into another ravine. At the head of this one was a crevice with a waterfall that splashed on the rocks around it. All modesty vanished. I pulled off my tee shirt. Reaching into the crevice, I rinsed it in the fresh, clear and deliciously cold water. I sucked the water from my shirt and then tended to my still bleeding leg. Before leaving the waterfall I soaked my shirt and pulled it over me, wet. It would keep me cool a little while.

On the ground I saw the cub's paw prints again. That was rare. I knew the travelers ahead of me were also refreshed. Then the cub's prints disappeared again and water filled the tracks of the mother bear. I felt safe trailing her until I reached the canyon.

On the ground her still dry tracks were facing me. The cub's prints indicated it had been wedged between its mother's sturdy front legs as she had watched me at the waterfall. There was no water in her prints, nor were there any bears in sight. I waited for their indentations to fill, listening to the thunderous song, enjoying the playful gusts of wind, and absorbing the commanding beauty that engulfed me.

Near the halfway point, the sound became deafening, but there was no more water or ice. I doggedly hiked in the bear's tracks toward the head of yet another ravine, the sides of which had a film of water running on the surface. It would've taken a long time to get enough moisture to have helped her, or me. I needed water to keep going. Both the ground and my legs shook. I started to sit down on one of the few wide spots I had encountered, to stop my legs from quivering, when I saw the water-filled hole. She had used her huge paws to dig a hole that was now filled with clear water. It seemed like she was helping me to survive. It became evident she was watching me from her tracks.

I soaked up my tee shirt in tepid water. It took a long while. As I sucked the water from my shirt I felt the strange bond that had been created between the bears and me.

The fine spray from the falls greeted us past the halfway point. Every time we cleared another scorching ravine, we were christened with the mist. The top of the canyon's walls were only a few feet above, and the trees were denser as they grew closer to the nourishing water of the falls.

The chilling mist drenched me. I painfully turned into an alcove abreast of the falls. In the muddy ground the mother bear's tracks faced me one last time. Up the gentle forested slopes her tracks and those of her cub faded into the bushes. A few tufts of fur and her tracks were all I had seen of her; she might have been an illusion. I crossed over the permanent barrier at the end of the trail. Looking up I could see the fading sunlight reflecting off the cars on the nearby road.

I sat on a fallen tree in silence and watched the white rushing water. The song of the falls did not enter this sheltered spot, although its thunder throbbed through the terrain. Was that a sound of breathing and a whine of a tired cub? As much as I wanted to see her, I didn't turn around. If she was studying me, I let her watch in anonymous safety.

"Thank you for being my angel," I whispered to the intimate solitude that wrapped protectively around me.

# Boathouse On The Bay

## Steve Rudis

The fisherman left his boathouse and slowly closed the door,
    too old to go to sea anymore.
Days were now  spent on the abandoned docks nestled in the bay,
Watching birds and children play.

He would travel into town and perhaps spend some time
    to visit an old flame who had also passed her prime.
Returning to the docks, to watch the birds and children play,
He carefully closed the door to his boathouse on the bay.

STEVE RUDIS

# Up the Chilkoot

Carl and Polski disembarked the steamship Goldwave and headed up the docks into Skagway, Alaska. The year was 1898 and the town was alive with gold fever.

Bars, sporting good stores and brothels constructed mainly of canvas tents lined Main Street. The two were looking for a place to stay for the night before heading to the Klondike gold fields. Their main obstacle, the deadly Chilkoot Pass, lay before them towering in the distance.

Carl and Polski walked along the wooden sidewalks and entered the Gold Dust Saloon. Miners were bellied up to the bar talking about their experiences in the gold fields across the border in Canada. The two made their way to a couple empty seats at the end of the bar and sat down next to Gold Pan Freddie. Freddie gave the two a once-over and quickly turned away, pretending not to notice the newcomers.

The two men ordered shots of whiskey as Carl asked the bartender, "Would you know of any place to stay for the night?" Freddie sipped from his glass of whiskey as Carl made his housing inquiry.

"Ya might ask Gold Pan Freddie sittin' next to ya," said the bartender, as he quickly moved away down to the middle of the bar to pour more drinks.

The two turned to the old miner with a long gray beard and Derby hat who was acting like he didn't hear the conversation. Carl and Polski introduced themselves and bought Freddie a drink as they pumped him for information about places to stay.

After downing a second drink, Freddie said, "You guys new in town?"

"Yup," both replied.

"What kind of work ya lookin' for?"

"Well, we thought we might try our hand in the gold fields after resting up in town for the night," replied Polski.

"Oh..." said Freddie, still playing naive. He went on to say, "Well, there's Nan's Nugget Hotel toward the end of town, but I don't think ya'd get much rest there — with all them ladies runnin' around the place all night." Freddie chuckled to himself. "Ya probably ought to try the Panhandle Hotel, just west off Main Street."

With that said, Gold Pan Freddie got off his bar stool, thanked the two newcomers for the drinks and disappeared out the back door of the saloon. No sooner did Freddie leave than another man sat down. After introductions, Howard began to tell Carl and Polski about his experience the first few days he spent in Skagway.

"I was told you could send a telegraph message back to Seattle," said Howard. "The only trouble is, there is no telegraph lines in this part of the country yet. It cost me five dollars, and when I went back to the telegraph office, the place was closed for remodeling."

Carl and Polski looked at each other, finished their drinks, and headed out the door to find the Panhandle Hotel. After finding a room, they dropped off their loaded backpacks. The two had brought some gear with them from Seattle and decided to buy a mule that afternoon from the local livery stable. The next morning at sunup the would-be miners headed toward the Chilkoot Pass.

Climbing the pass was a long and arduous feat. Along the way, Carl and Polski saw the remains of parties that were less fortunate. Skeletal remains of pack animals and smashed gear could be seen in some of the canyons below them as they climbed ever higher along the perilous trail. Finally, they reached the top and admired the magnificent view of the mountain pass as they took a well-deserved rest.

As they rested, a miner approached from the opposite direction, returning from the Klondike gold fields and heading toward Skagway. His face wore a disappointed look as he stopped to talk with Carl and Polski.

"When I got to Dawson in the Yukon Territory, I found that most of the good gold claims were already staked," the discouraged miner explained. "I managed to find a few nuggets, but that was about it. Some guys ended up working for people who had claims, but I decided to head on back. See ya," said the ex-miner as he headed on down the trail.

Carl and Polski thought their world had just caved in. Their dreams of getting rich by just getting to the gold fields had evaporated with just a few words from the disillusioned miner. The two sat silently for a few moments before Polski said, "Well, we've made it this far, so why not keep going anyway?"

"Why not?" replied Carl. "At least we can say that we been there."

The two looked south one more time, then turned and headed north with their trusty pack mule trailing behind.

# Pipe Dreams

(Humor)

*Devise, wit; write, pen;*
*for I am for whole volumes in folio.*
*—Shakespeare*

PATRICIA LAWTON

# Chickens I Have Known:
## (Especially You, Mergatroid)

Ah Mergatroid, where do I start? In the beginning I guess. My first encounter with chickens was when my uncle would take me out to the coop to collect the eggs. I was four years old. I remember reaching under the hens into the warm straw to find the eggs — that is, if they would let me. My uncle found it incredibly funny when they would peck at me. I still like the smell of a chicken coop; of course I also like the smell of gasoline fumes.

That same year one of my friends announced that his mother was going to chop off the head of one of their chickens. We all ran to watch. We climbed up on the fence to get a clear view. I remember the chopping block and the loop she put over the chicken's head. It tried to escape but to no avail. Down came the ax, and away it ran minus one important part.

We went in to have Kool-Aid — cherry of course. Through the kitchen window I could see the chicken still running, stumbling, and getting up again. My friend's mother explained that it was just nerves. It couldn't feel anything.

Well, in my opinion that chicken was still aware that something just wasn't right.

For many years I didn't encounter any one chicken in particular that was as memorable. Unless you count the yellow fuzzy ones with the orange-wrapped legs in the Easter baskets.

About fifteen years later, my mom started gathering unusual chickens to raise, and you, Mergatroid, were one of them. You were having a hard time hatching. My mother said that farm women would nestle eggs in their ample bosoms to keep them warm. "Well," I said, "I can do that." She looked at me doubtfully. It was in the sixties, but I did wear a bra. With you tucked safely inside my shirt, off we marched to the K-Mart with my two-year-old daughter in tow. That day the store had a lot of blue-light specials. Needless to say, you decided it was time to enter the world. As I waited in line, your peeps grew louder and louder. I confessed to the sales clerk what I was doing. Mind you, my daughter was only two, but she still remembers the scene at the checkout stand. I guess there are some things you shouldn't say in public.

I took you home where you grew into a fine specimen. You had rich green bronze and gold feathers. You liked to bite the hands that fed you or spur the legs of your benefactors. No one wanted an ill-mannered rooster. The decision was made to end your time here, prematurely. I didn't want your head chopped off. My husband considered himself a marksman and agreed to shoot you with his 22-caliber rifle. I went into the house. Three shots later, I ran out. There you were running back and forth like a rabbit in a shooting gallery. I screamed, "I hate you," at my husband and ran horrified back into the house. One more shot rang out. I didn't want to see you, and I certainly wasn't going to eat you. My husband said he would take care of everything.

My husband had ordered a fly-tying kit earlier in the year. A month or two after the unpleasant end of you, Mergatroid, my husband proudly showed me some flies he had been tying. They looked good; I was impressed; they looked familiar. They were rich green bronze and gold. Could he be so callous? Upon closer examination, they were definitely miniature replicas of you.

You know what, Mergatroid? You brought it on yourself. If you hadn't been such a dumb cluck, this story would have had a different ending.

MICHAEL ROBBINS

# New Hombre in Town

T en days in a bumpy stagecoach would be enough to rile any
man. Tack on the constant throb in his stump and it was
small wonder Wiley stepped off the stage in a cross mood.
Naturally the once-a-year rain would begin to fall at this par-
ticular time. It pecked spots in the dry earth and steamed from the
rooftops. Idlewood was a typical tin-pan town. It had been born on a
rumor and most likely would die once the mines played out.

Yet it was also a way station for pilgrims. Farmers came for new
lands to plow; card sharks, newlyweds, and widowers came too, all
carrying nothing but a bag of hope on their backs.

Wiley could've had his pick of any job east of Independence. He
also knew he'd have quit inside of a week. Wiley chose Idlewood
because the plain truth was he couldn't abide quiet. As he passed by
a saloon, one of a dozen he spotted in town, a wrangler flopped in
Wiley's path like a warped chunk of timber, raising small plumes of
dust around his sprawled limbs. Wiley stepped across him with a
nod. This town would be agreeable.

The letter Wiley carried instructed him to meet his contact on
the stoop of Fireman Bob's Barbershop. And there he was, frock-
coated arms raised to the sky. Behind him a flock of parishioners
swooned over the pistol waving in the hand of a bandito wearing
heavy bandoliers.

Hmmph! Greenhorns. Well, he aimed to bring civility to
Idlewood. Might as well start here.

Wiley hefted a book from his black bag. Good solid spine, he
observed. Then he whacked the bandito square in the noggin,
mashing his sombrero down across his eyes.

Wiley snagged one shoulder, turned the man about, and smacked the leatherbound tome into his whiskered cheek. The fellow landed in the door of Fireman Bob's Barbershop.

A long-faced old timer wearing an apron and stripes peered around the corner. "I expect you'd be the barber or the coroner." Wiley said, and nodded toward the fallen bandito. "Either way he needs a shave," he said.

Then he presented his credentials to his contact, who gulped as he unfolded the bundle of papers. "Brethren," he called to the crowd and pointed to Wiley. "May I present our new pastor!"

# Mohave Madness

"**N**o doubt about it, Tom, there is desert in my blood (along with the Irish)," I said to myself as we headed out. Another April. Another convention for me and old Art.

I was driving my new camper rig with Art beside me. As usual, he was trying to put words into all the quiet spaces. My mind was racing ahead to tomorrow and my opening address at the first general session. To what? To whom? Eight or nine thousand delegates? In another few miles I would give that a rest and muse about the other things in my blood: flying, rock hunting, fly fishing, drinking some, and sitting around telling lies.

There's never enough time for everything, though. Now that I'm in the upper echelon of education (did I say that?), my "comp time" is piled up on me and I know it's because I just can't let go.

Take right now. This trip to Las Vegas. It is not one of your ordinary going-off-to-Las Vegas-to-gamble-must-have-been-saving-up-some-money-for-it kind of trip. This is convention business as usual, or almost — meetings, speeches, exhibits, hospitality suites, and story telling — as much as I can cut through smoke-filled rooms.

A trip to Las Vegas is always a gamble. But for me, it will not be money changing hands to the advantage of the house. I need to get away for a little adventure. In the desert. While I'm here on the Mojave.

When we got to Las Vegas and had moved into the room we would share, I said to Art, "Before all the action starts tomorrow I'll just slip out into the desert for the night and find out if the camper is comfortable and all it is supposed to be. I'll see you tomorrow morning at the first general session."

So off I went into the Nevada desert, feeling more like the way I used to feel knocking around eastern Oregon among the rattlesnakes and the sage brush, hunting rocks — mostly with Uncle Timothy. Funny guy, but he taught me almost everything I know about the out-of-doors. Now I'm on my own, always waiting for a chance to get out in it.

As I drove I tried to take in everything I saw. The desert flowers were coming into bloom. Several times I stopped to take pictures of cactus and talk to the critters. The brown of the desert, now brightening to green, was turning to purple as daylight faded to dusk.

I drove for miles and miles to get away from it all in my head. When I felt hungry, I stopped at a roadside cafe. It was packed with folks eating and drinking, but I found a table for one and gave the waitress a nod for a drink to get things started.

What happened then was hardly what I had in mind. The waitress and I understood each other. But what of this stranger who sidled over to my table, and drew up a chair and planted his elbows? He looked into my face before we had exchanged words, then he ordered a beer and launched into a monologue about himself, his troubles mostly, with both men and women. He waved to the waitress to refill my glass, and asked, "Where you headed?"

"Thought I'd do some camping, try out my new rig," I told him.

"Why camp?" he asked, draining his glass and waving for a refill. "There's a campground right down the road, sure, but I'm staying in a cabin 'cross the road from it."

I was beginning to wonder about this guy's extraordinary hospitality. So I stood up and said I had to be going.

"Stop by the cabin for a nightcap then," he said, getting to his feet and walking me to the door. That didn't seem like a bad idea at the time.

At his cabin we continued the drinks and his monologue. Finally, as if I had initiated something, which I had not, the guy said, "I hate to see you go off to the campground," and he began making his moves. It was too early for dawn, but it dawned right then. I knew I was in a hurry to leave.

"Hey," I told him, "I just realized how late it is and how little time I have for setting up camp anyway. And then I have to make a speech at eight o'clock in the morning. Guess I'll just run back into Las Vegas and be done with it."

The guy covered his disappointment well, but followed me out. He watched me get into my rig and haul myself out of there, not in

the direction of the campground, but back toward Las Vegas.
I drove and drove, retracing the miles, hoping to find a campground
I had missed on the way out. But what could I expect? How many
campgrounds are there in the Stove Pipe Wells neighborhood?

I circled back through the dusk which had turned to dark, past
the guy's cabin as if I had never been down that road before, and
turned into the campground, just across from his cabin, as he had
said. There was no sign of the man.

Darkness had taken over my rig, but I kept going. The dark blue
sky filled with stars, beautiful as it was, afforded me no light at all.
Peering into the dark I could tell I had my choice of campsite, but I
drove as far into the campground as I could go — just in case the
man had followed me after all. At the far end of the campground
there were two spaces, one taken up by a Volkswagen camper bus
and a small tent. There was no light over there, but after all that had
happened I was glad to be alone at last.

I pulled in, locked up the cab, climbed into the camper, stripped
down ready to crawl into my bag, then I checked the door. It was
still too warm to shut up tight. I left the door ajar.

As I lay there, I thought about the week ahead: the meetings,
the socializing. It made me weary thinking about it, but it felt good
lying there in the quiet.

It seemed as if I had just fallen asleep when I was roused by
sounds I could not identify. Nor could I remember where I was.
Oh…of course…practically in Death Valley. Listening did not clear
up the mystery, nor did it satisfy my curiosity.

I sat up and drew aside one of the curtains. In the heavy gray of
early dawn I saw the little tent next to the Volkswagen gyrating as if
giant wrestlers were embattled to pin one or the other. "I'll be go-to-
hell, I haven't seen that since our family used to camp when I was a
boy, all eight of us kids and Mother and Dad. Their tent used to
shake like that."

By that time I was too wide awake to lie down again. May as
well get on the road. I dressed quickly, moved to the door which was
no longer ajar. It must have drifted shut while I slept. I gave a turn
to the handle but nothing happened. I gave it a jerk and nearly tore
my arm off. My whole body careened into the door when it didn't
open.

What's this? Didn't I try out everything before I drove off the
sales lot with this rig? Guess not. I looked it over carefully, tried
putting pressure on the lock and lifting. Before I panicked com-

pletely, I remembered why I was awake so early.

I took another look out the window toward the little tent. Things had sort of settled down over there. Maybe that man from last night could help me out. I definitely needed to get out and be on my way.

It seemed like an eerie thing to do, but I had to get help. So I called out, "Help me out of here!" All commotion subsided over there, but that was all that happened. Maybe they hadn't heard me. I tried again. "I can't get out! Over here!"

More happened then that I had expected. A man pulling on his drawers I thought, although it was hard to be sure in the half-light, opened the tent flap. But he sprinted to the V-dub, unlocked it and slid open the side door. Back to the tent he went.

In seconds he burst out again, rolling up a sleeping bag or two — probably zipped together. He threw the bags into the bus. On the next fast trip he hauled out an inflated air mattress, now slowly losing air, and threw that into the bus.

I hoped to get his attention on one of those panic bursts, so I called out, as calmly as possible, trying not to sound as if I were calling from the grave, "My door won't open. Can you help me out?"

On the next trip to the bus, his arms were full of shoes and pieces of clothing, but it did seem as if he had heard me. Just before he collapsed the tent, the woman stepped out and made a quick run to the bus. He stuffed the tent in on top of all the gear and was about to jump into the driver's seat when he must have thought better of it. Without any sign of acknowledgement, one human being to another human being, he covered the distance to my door in determined giant strides. He grabbed the handle of my door, gave it a twist, and forced it to open.

It was his one fast move to rescue a dying desert rat that he didn't know and didn't want to know. He didn't wait for a word of thanks. He turned and ran, jumped into the bus, and drove off, spinning his wheels in the desert sand.

Really alone now, I thought about all the things that had happened to me in the last twelve hours. There was no hurry now. There was no danger of dying like the prospectors of gold rush days in Death Valley.

Now that it was over, it occurred to me that it might be fun telling about my adventure back at the meetings. Of course everyone would say, "Just another one of Tom's stories..." They did say it. But I got their attention. So what the hell!

170

James Francis Smith

# The Perils of E-mail

From: tahoe@att.net
To: sligum@pacificrain.net
Subject: Snow and bear bound.
Hi,
We've been trapped in our cabin for over a week. A
California black bear decided to hibernate beneath
our deck. We called the sheriff who promised to
bring the animal control unit, but a thirty-two-
inch snowfall prevented them from reaching our
remote location. Thank God, we have a cozy fire,
sufficient food and a fully stocked liquor cabinet.

    Would you please take a peek at our house and
make sure that everything is all right. We'll see you
in the spring.

The Rafts.


From: sligum@pacificrain.net
To: tahoe@att.net
Subject: Stay Snowbound
I'm sorry to hear about your troubles with the bear. I hope it's a he
and not a she. I've been told that once a she-bear selects a home, she
never leaves. Please e-mail me and let me know how you make out. I
mean about the bear, not whether you and Charlie get bare and
make out. (A little joke to take your mind off your troubles.) I'm
sorry to hear that you are stuck down in Tahoe until spring. The
people that t.p.ed your house are probably sorry as well. It rained the
next day and the place is a mess. It'll probably be spring before the

t.p. dries anyway. I think that the only way you'll get the t.p. out of the fir trees is cut several down. If you want, I'll hire a tree cutter and get them started right away.

I wouldn't worry about the drunk who drove across your lawn. After all, he missed the house. A little topsoil, some seed and in time things will look the same. In fact, a person can hardly notice anything wrong since the grass hasn't been cut for months. I hope you haven't pre-paid the lawn maintenance fellow because I heard he ran away with your next door neighbor's wife.

Back to the drunk, things wouldn't have been so bad if the local cops hadn't followed him so closely and crashed into your garage door. It sure scared the hell out of the moles. I did find someone who agreed to take that antique car off your hands — the one you've been restoring these past five years. He offered a hundred and fifty dollars which, based on the looks of the wreck, seems fair. However, he wants to pay in penny stock. If I were you, with the way the stock market's crashing, I'd demand at least half of it in good hard cash.

Which reminds me, I attended the funeral of your stockbroker last week. It seems that the poor fellow absconded with all his clients' funds, lost everything while gambling in Reno, and committed suicide rather than face the wrath of some very angry customers. So much for your 401k fund. It's a good thing he bailed out of the market before the latest downturn or else he wouldn't have had anything to gamble. I've been told that he made some very bad stock selections and would have been wiped out had he remained in the market. Isn't Reno near your cabin? Maybe if you weren't snowed in, you could have given him some tips on gambling.

I understand the tree from your neighbor's yard that tumbled across your deck didn't do much damage either. Of course, the tree will have to be removed before we know for certain. The squirrels seem to be grateful; a branch poked a hole into your siding and the furry animals established a colony there.

Don't let the rumors about a mud slide bother you. The back and side fence can easily be repaired after the tons of soggy dirt are finally removed. However, the water building up behind the mudslide may become a problem. The township claims it's not their responsibility and the adjoining neighbors have brought a suit against you. Fortunately, the judge delayed hearing the suit until the dam bursts and the final tally of damages can be ascertained.

There is some good news. The car you left behind has been located. At least we think that's the case. The extensive damage makes it impossible to be certain that it belongs to you. That may be in your favor because the parking lot owner wants to collect the full amount due for the extensive time the car occupied his lot. Let's pray that next time a car thief will choose a less expensive location to stow a stolen vehicle.

Who would have thought that short-lived cold spell would freeze your pipes and cause all that water damage in your rec room. By stepping carefully, someone can avoid the deepest puddles and make their way to the bathroom and bedrooms. Of course, getting to the bathroom doesn't do much good because the toilet is stopped up and the plumber slipped coming down the stairs and broke a disk in his back. He swears that you will hear from him. Which is a rarity, because few of us ever hear from a plumber once we agree to his estimate. I'm certain that the odor from the sewage that backed up will dissipate in time.

I hope you didn't leave any valuables behind because we discovered that someone broke down your new front doors. It's difficult to tell what's missing because almost everything is gone. There is one blessing: nothing was taken from downstairs. Even a burglar wouldn't wade through that dank clutter.

I can't tell you much about the fire since the engines were leaving when we arrived. The neighbors think a vagrant domiciled in your bedroom may have tossed a lit cigarette into the pile of overdue bills accumulating on your porch. We rescued all the mail that we could, including the notification that your fire insurance had been cancelled. Among the pieces were the late payment notice for your property taxes, a tax lien and the notice from the county threatening to auction off your property. Don't think you have to rush home for the auction, it took place last week. I tried to mail the remains of your overdue bills that we recovered, but the post office refused to accept them. I'm not really clear on the reason; however, there was white ash seeping from the envelope, so it may have something to do with the anthrax scare.

I do hope things work out between you and the bear. Lord knows life is difficult enough without a tussle with one of Mother Nature's creatures. Take care of yourselves and have a safe and pleasant trip home.

The Smiths

# Crossed Words

## Jacqueline Dock

Little empty squares
Wait for me.
Pencil across, pen down.

"Ram's ma'am"?     EWE!
"Horse's halter"?     WHOA!
"Bear's hair"?     FUR!

The letters march in,
But still there are holes.
I open the crossword dictionary.
The solution is not there.

"Head light"?     HALO!
"Night light"?     NEON!
"Bad lighting"?     ARSON!

I leave the puzzle
And return later.
Now the words jump into place.

"A train"?     BCDEF!
"Union Jack"?     DUES!
"It's all over ewe"?     WOOL!

Stacks of words pile up
Outside the grid
Waiting to be used.

"1-2-3, 1-2-3 …"?        WALTZ!
"Am _ _____"?            AM I BLUE!
"Fodder for sheep"?
Little lambs eat         IVY!

Now I have a word,
My crossed words have created a word
I do not recognize,
A word not in the dictionary;
My error, or the puzzle's creator?

"Lazy woman"?            SUSAN!
"Happy companion"?       DOG!
"Second story man"?      LIAR!

What a sense of humor!
An ex headline writer?

"I lid"?                 DOT!
"Man over board"?        SURFER!

Now I am stuck:

"I __ O N"?

The cross clue is

"Dr. Seuss' 'If I _____ the Zoo'"?

Aah, until tomorrow
When little empty squares…

# Googly Time
## DAN SLOAN

Amnok glibed the deedle bop,
While Enos wold my scrunge.
For weedle must forendo gump
And defren will be bunge.
We all defer the end of jop,
And we all regrunge the glibe.
The googlies don't free ano slump
But do core enjo nibe.

Hablee gebunk and reno stiles
Dement and anno strup,
Weldnet for Amok's weedle fram
Rejoice for Enos' glup.
Behold the rising hidle smiles
It's really wee wee snork,
I like the winter's framistam
And summer's really spork.

I will not hoard the wheedle dee
I will not hangle slick.
But I will always goofy foot
The rolling platy stick,
And frequently will deedle whee
When I should upper cut
And then I'll en me alli put
And wildly wonker mutt.

All joyously and all friendly be
The time has come to whoop.
The end of quagly goonis ton
Marks well the wetted stoop.
Anon the mighty maple tree
Extends its mighty arm
To carry all the leaves thereon
And shade us all from harm.

From this I learned to gluggly poo
In time to fordiluck.
I like now to giggle free
I like to gimbly suck
I now will quickly hang a new
Free tonic frang a whang
The world will never rumple me
While I still gag a bang.

JULIE JENNINGS

# The Giant's View

What's all this blather about Jack being a hero? You know, why doncha all stand back a little and actually see Jack for the pipsqueak liar he is. Come to think of it, Jack's one of the laziest people around. Guess he thinks he's better than the rest of us and doesn't see the need to work. Heck, I work — help my wife make meals, keep house and grow a fantastic garden of vegetables.

Jack's a simpleton born of poor stock. He hasn't even a horse's ass for a brain. I mean really, who in their right mind would sell a cow for beans just because they're pretty? And to boot, that family was starving. You see, I take care of my own. No one goes hungry here; but he lets his own mother down, although the mother seems just as foolish. There she is, hungry, without a cow, but she has beans that could make many meals — bean soup, bean bread, baked beans and so much more. So what does she go and do? She throws those beans out the window. She could've thrown them in a pot of hot water and had a meal.

Now, get this: the next morning there's a beanstalk to my castle. That stupid Jack finds enough energy to climb up and invade my palace. Yet, he can't work or listen to his mother? What's with that disrespect? Jack lies to people about a woman who warns him that I'm evil. Well, God Almighty, what does he think trespassing is? To tell you the truth, I have a giant heart and don't mind sharing — when one is invited.

His lying shows great imagination, one that is useful only in wriggling and squirming his way out of truth. What God-given right does this boy have to trespass into my home and hide? Of course I smelled the boy in time, but his smell was mixed with too many with cooking smells.

I eat while my wife brings me Henrietta my pet hen. I stroke her feathers and asked her to lay. The hen plops out a giant golden egg. I pat Henrietta along with my full belly, and promptly fall asleep.

I awake to wild squawking. "Little thief," I roar. I want to scare the little weasel into dropping the hen, so I roar some more, "Fee fi fo fum, I smell the blood of an Englishman." He slides down the beanstalk lickety split!

The next day I ponder how to make my house secure. More servants, maybe one of those grand security alarm systems. No, I decide. He won't be back, not after the fright I gave him. Boy was I wrong. He sneaks in again. I smell him stronger this time, still not enough to catch the little thief.

So I eat, grumpily thumping my foot. I mean wouldn't you be upset at a trespasser? I need consolation and call my harp to play. Music, soothing…ah…to these ears. Finally, I'm soothed into rest, and shut my eyes, for what…a moment? The little twerp has stolen my harp. Since when are thieves heroes?

He's gonna pay! I stomp after him, and plan to hold him until the Giant Police come and book him into custody for two counts trespassing and two counts first degree theft. But no, the slippery slime slides down the beanstalk again. I'm halfway down when he whacks the beanstalk twice and I crash unceremoniously to the ground. I can hear them as I start to fade into darkness.

The town yells, "The evil giant is dead, hurrah, hurrah!" So I guess murder, destruction of property and stolen goods mean nothing to anyone. Hero? My giant butt.

"Would somebody make sure that Jack gets what he deserves? And please take care of my wife? I'm fading."

180

Thomas J. Martin

# It's Their Fathers

In the early eighties, as I grew into being a man, I often heard others complain about mothers-in-law with the same tired old jokes and one-liners. Perhaps the problems with a mate's mother may be relevant only in marriage, or perhaps the originators of the myths never lived in a semi rural area, but I found it was the fathers of the girls I dated who gave me the most problems.

I definitely won't forget Annette's father. In her case, with her mother gone, the mother-in-law or the potential mother-in-law issue was irrelevant. Her father, a tough rugged man, then working for a new high technology company, looked ideal as a future father-in-law.

A friendly man, popular, and a big muscular fellow with a sense of humor, he welcomed me warmly enough, throwing out his hand when I came over the first time to pick up his daughter for our date. He found out from Annette that I played football in high school, which I barely did, having neither talent nor size, but that was enough to give me an in.

I endured football. The coach in practice generally used me when the star players were tired of running around pylons and when the monsters on the team needed something softer to hit than the tackling dummies. I think they didn't cut me because they happened to have a set of new small pads and jerseys wasting shelf space, or else they enjoyed seeing me fly after getting blocked, which upped the confidence of the real players.

For my part, I played mainly so that in later life I could nod knowingly when the topic of team sports came up in bars and at work, and I figured time would gloss over my being swatted about the field and stepped on with sickening regularity.

I also played football so I could go out with girls like Annette. Of course I shared none of this with Annette's dad when he talked about his glory days; I just nodded knowingly.

While Annette was "getting ready" (something he told me that I wanted to question since I'd seen her standing with her jacket on, holding her purse, ready when I came in), he took me to see his gun collection.

Oh, great, male bonding, I figured, not having any interest in guns. I was much more interested in checking out Annette, who joined us wearing a new dress and dangly earrings, my greatest weakness. She beckoned me more than oily metal and wood. She looked at me with sad encouragement in those hazel eyes as I stepped away from her to put up with a rite of passage or screening, or whatever awaited me in the paneled room. His expression worried me greatly — a grin. I glumly followed him into the den, forcing a manly smile on my own face.

There I saw pictures, many pictures, of dead animals with him grinning above them — either standing, kneeling, or squatting — and holding some sinister steel and wood weapon that had taken the same unfortunate fur-bearing or feathered creature at his feet. A few stuffed animals with glass eyes stared accusingly from their rigid crouches in the corners. With a pride he should have reserved for introducing his daughter, he showed me several of his firearms. Most of them looked alike to me, but I remembered two of them.

He handed me something called a 300 Win-Mag or some such, with which he'd "dropped a beautiful elk at over five hundred yards." I wanted to ask him why he'd kill something that was beautiful. I would prefer to look at something beautiful, like his daughter, and I'd sure not want to hurt her. Of course, I didn't say anything as I numbly held the heavy rifle, which I figured was worth a great deal more then my beater car.

He then showed me an over and under shotgun, with which he said he could snap shoot quail and pheasant consistently. I joked, a bit acerbically, that it would be a fine item to have on hand if attacks by quail and pheasant on human beings became more frequent. He missed my point, laughed out loud and slapped me solidly on my shoulder.

Since I obviously was just displaying polite interest, I began to wonder why he showed me his firearms at all — until we started to leave. He placed his hand on my shoulder and squeezed a bit too hard to be friendly, made Clint Eastwood-type eye contact and gave me a second to ensure he had my full attention.

"Be good to my daughter." He smiled seriously at me.

I had Annette home by eleven that night.

K imberly lived off a country road, a bit of a drive away. I don't remember what her father did for a living, but I know he drank beer professionally and was a gruff, rugged type. I went over to pick her up one day with high hopes for a successful evening. At school she was a pretty young woman who didn't smile and said little. I hoped to get her to open up and tell me what she was really like.

I drove up to her house past the barbed wire on both sides of the road and saw a pick-up truck parked in the yard with a shotgun rack in the rear window and a bumper sticker that proclaimed the vehicle was "Insured by Smith and Wesson" — and I assumed by no one else. Great, I thought as I walked up the gravel and mud driveway. I worried slightly about my expensive shoes as I walked past an enormous bear-killing dog barking insanely.

"Don't worry, Cujo ain't bit no one in over a month," called out Kimberly's mother, from the partially open screen door. "Now don't you look nice," she added, as I briskly stepped up on the porch.

I dressed for the occasion — a play — in a manner that was stylish then. I wore a striped shirt, a solid knit tie, pleated trousers, and a Members Only leather jacket. I walked through the door into a world of flannel shirts, shotguns, and Budweiser.

Kimberly's dad was sitting in an easy chair watching a ball game on television and cleaning a shotgun. He had another pump action beside him, likely loaded, and a pile of empty Bud cans impressively stacked before him. He wore a baseball cap decorated with a crude innuendo involving fishermen's rods, earning him the honor of being the first person I've ever seen wear that kind of hat. I noticed his lumberjack shirt, blue jeans, and muddy boots.

Butch, Kimberly's brother, twenty-four or twenty-five years old and still living at home without a girlfriend or a solid job, also wore a flannel shirt, his sleeves torn off exposing his crudely inked "Death from Above" tattoo. I found this amusing, since he never served in the Army, much less the Airborne, or had done much of anything. Butch was cleaning a Winchester while smirking at me.

"Sit down, Boy," grunted Kimberly's dad, nodding toward a chair covered with oil-soaked gun cleaning rags and issues of Motor Trend and the American Rifleman.

I sat down.

"Look at this fella, Butch, all decked out to take out your little sister," he said and glared at me. Butch snorted.

"Damn, Kid, there ain't much girth to you, is there?" he continued. I figured that if they started talking about how many pennies a pound I was worth, I was going back out with Cujo.

"Where ya takin' my daughter?" he demanded, turning down the TV's volume.

"To see a play at the college. A lot of people I know are in it," I replied.

"A play! What kinda prissy-assed date is that?" asked Kimberly's brother. Her father raised his hand for silence from Butch, then nodded toward me. "Good 'nuff," he said. He looked a bit relaxed. "That's fine as long as you don't get any odd notions with Kimmee."

Notions? I'd never heard it called that before. We sat silently for a while.

"That's a mighty fine leather jacket, so at least you ain't one of them animal lovers," Her dad said, grabbing a beer from one of the many that floated on the ice in a five-gallon bucket near his foot.

"So, did you knit the tie yourself?" asked Butch. He and his father burst out laughing. I wanted to ask him if he did that pathetic tattoo himself, but I decided for some reason to be polite and bite my tongue.

Butch grabbed a beer, then nudged his father and gestured toward me with the beer can.

"Trick question, Son. You wanna beer?" asked her father in a serious, level tone.

Damn! I was way underage, about to drive his daughter a good distance just to get to civilization, yet they were offering me a beer. If I turned it down, they might think I was snubbing them. If I drank it, they might figure I was irresponsible. The room was silent. Even Butch stopped wiping down his Winchester as they awaited my answer. I admit I wondered whether the answer would mean my date with Kimberly would be called off or something much worse would happen.

Kimberly saved my butt by saying to her mother, "But, Mom, I like this one."

Her mother walked up to Kim's father and said that we had to get on the road in order to be on time for the play.

On the way out, I didn't even care when I stepped in a muddy puddle up to my ankle. I figured then that this wasn't going to go too far, and I was sure as hell going to have her back by eleven.

A short time later, I met Marie. We seemed to hit it right off. But one of the first questions I asked her was whether or not her father hunted and collected guns. She said no.

I married her.

Then I found out about mothers-in-law.

# THE CHRISTMAS BAT CAROL

### Submitted by Dan Sloan

### Janice Sloan lyricist

(Sung to the tune of "Santa Claus Is Coming to Town")

Verse 1:
Two large dark wings blot out the light
Of that famed eastern star.
It is the jolly Christmas Bat
Spreading greetings near and far.

Refrain:
*You better not cry, you better not pout,*
*You better not stick your jugular vein out,*
*Christmas Bat is coming to town.*

Verse 2:
He has such lovely canine teeth.
They are so strong and white.
You'll see his smiling greeting
If you are out on Christmas Night.

Verse 3:
Flapping down the chimney,
In each stocking he will peek.
If you wear a low-necked Christmas gown,
You may find you've sprung a leak.

Verse 4:
He knows if you've been sleeping;
He knows if you're awake;
He knows if you taste bad or good,
So taste BAD for goodness sake!

Verse 5:
He loves the Christmas colors,
The green and red, I mean.
If he gets to your rich red blood,
You'll turn a lovely Christmas green.

# Sweet Dreams

## (For Children)

*I never knew so young a body
with so old a head.*
*—Shakespeare*

DONNA ANDERSON

# Brownie Bear

Brownie Bear shouted, "I'm hungry!" and then he growled — very loud. He wasn't mad, he just felt like growling. Brownie Bear just woke up from his long winter's nap. It is called hibernating. Sleeping can make you hungry, and Brownie Bear woke up very hungry. After all, he'd been asleep for four months.

Brownie stood at the door of his cave and started to remember the way things had been before he went to sleep. He remembered the tall trees. He remembered the warm sun. He remembered the big lake. He remembered the many fish in the lake. And then he remembered he was very hungry.

Brownie walked down to the lake. The sun felt warm, but there were still snow patches on the ground, and the lake's frozen top was just starting to melt. The fish were there too, but they were frozen in the ice. It didn't take very long for Brownie to drag these frozen fishcicles to the bank and onto his favorite sunning rock. He had three fish ready for breakfast. "But wait a minute," he thought. "If I get three more, I will have enough for lunch too."

Off he went to find fish. Brownie found three more fish in the ice and brought them back to the sunning rock. Now he had enough for breakfast and lunch.

Once again he thought, "If I get three more, I wouldn't have to catch any fish until tomorrow, and I could just lie in the sun today and eat."

That sounded so good he was off again. This time he had to go farther down the shore. When he finally got back with the extra fish, he was tired — and still hungry. He added these to the fish on the sunning rock and sat down to rest. "I have enough fish for today, but if I just had three more fish, I would really be set. I could sleep late tomorrow and still have a good breakfast."

This time he went much farther. He went around the bend.

While he was gone to get the extra fish that he really didn't need, the fish on that warm rock began to thaw. This gave off a nice dinner smell to Mr. Wolf and his friends.

Mr. Wolf crept down to inspect the wonderful aroma and found all those fish on the sunning rock. Of course, the law of the forest is "finders-keepers," so...he called in his wolf friends and they carried off Brownie's fish.

When Brownie finally came back, he was really, really tired and he was really, really, really hungry. There had been no more fish to find. "Oh well," he thought, "I will just eat now and then take a nap." He went over to his sunning rock and found that all his fish were gone.

Brownie let out another big growl! This time he was angry. His greed had kept him away just long enough for the wolves to take everything. Brownie was disappointed, but then he remembered one more thing. His mother always said, "He who wants too much, loses all." His Mother had told him his greed would get him into trouble.

He didn't understood it before; now he did. Do you?

CHARLOTTE RICHARDS

# The Gold Weathercock

The courthouse in Sunnydale was old, almost as old as the town itself. It had been built when the first settlers began to move west. For many years the townspeople had been setting their watches by the big clock in the clock tower. For as many years, they had been predicting the weather by looking at the weather vane perched high up on top of the tower.

Auric the weathercock had once been young and strong and his body had gleamed a bright gold in the sunshine. When he first took up his perch, he was christened Auric because the name means "golden." His plumage was now tarnished and some of his proud tail feathers had broken off. Even though he was old and no longer handsome, he still stood erect upon his perch and proudly performed his task of showing the direction of the wind.

In recent years a family of swallows had made their home under the eaves of the building. Each spring Fleetwing, the father swallow, brought his wife back to Sunnydale to raise another brood of youngsters.

Auric and Fleetwing soon become fast friends. Each morning Fleetwing flew up to Auric's perch to tell him the latest town gossip. Auric repaid him by warning the swallow family of the approach of the courthouse cat.

The day finally came when Auric began to feel jealous of Fleetwing. For years he had been standing alone in all kinds of weather and now his joints were becoming stiff. Each year he found it more difficult to turn in different directions to show which way the wind was blowing.

But his friend had a warm cozy nest under the eaves which he shared with his loving family. Fleetwing also was handsome and graceful and liked to show off by swooping in daring loop-the-loops around the clock tower.

Auric thought, *If I were young and strong, I would be more than a match for that show-off Fleetwing*. When Fleetwing flew up to Auric's perch for his daily visit, Auric pretended to be too busy to talk to him.

"My friend," said Fleetwing, "what have I done to make you treat me like this?" But Auric did not answer.

When Fleetwing returned to his nest under the eaves, he complained to his wife, "Auric has always been my friend, but now he treats me like an enemy. What have I done wrong?"

His wife's answer was wise. "Your only fault is that you are young and handsome, while he is old and ugly. He is unable to forgive you your youth and vigor."

Far from being angry with his friend, Fleetwing began to think of ways to help Auric regain his former pride. Saying nothing to his wife, he began gathering up feathers of different colors. His friends gave what they could spare. There were blue feathers from the jays, red from the cardinals, and yellow from the orioles. From his own shiny plumage, Fleetwing plucked glossy black feathers. When he had gathered enough, he proudly presented them to Auric to hide his dull color.

With scorn, Auric threw the feathers away. They scattered like bright flowers over the rooftops. "Do you think I want to look like a parrot? If I wore these I would be the laughingstock of the town." Swinging around on his perch, he turned his back on Fleetwing.

The swallow was speechless with hurt over the unkind words of his friend. He flew back to his home and resolved never to help the ungrateful weathercock again.

That night, while everyone slept, a storm swept over the town and began to unleash its fury. Thunder rumbled and lightning lit up the sky. In the glow from the lightning flashes, Auric could be seen braving the storm from his perch.

Suddenly, at the height of the storm, a bolt of lightning struck Auric and nearly knocked him down from the top of the clock tower. His feathers were blackened and his head spun from the shock. Although almost blinded from the flash, he noticed that sparks from the lightning bolt had landed on the courthouse roof near the swallows' home. Little tongues of flame began creeping over the wooden shingles.

Auric's jealousy toward his friend was immediately forgotten.

"Fire, Fleetwing, fire!" he shouted in his rusty voice. "Save yourself and your family! The roof is burning!"

The swallows, who had been huddled under the eaves, tumbled hastily out of their nest and flew off to safety in the darkness. Soon torrents of water from the fire fighters' huge hoses quenched the flames.

In the days that followed, carpenters nailed new shingles on the roof. Auric's lightning- blackened body was covered with a new coat of shiny gold paint. Soon he gleamed with his original splendor. But even though his former beauty had been restored, he was unhappy. He would gladly have traded all his fine gold paint for a word from his friend.

He thought with sadness, *How cruel it was for me to treat Fleetwing so badly. If only I hadn't let jealousy destroy our friendship.*

One day after Auric had given up hope of ever seeing his old friend again, the swallows came back to their home under the eaves. Soon after their return, Fleetwing flew up to the top of the clock tower to greet Auric.

"It's good to see you again, dear friend. My family and I can never repay you for saving our lives. Forgive me for not thanking you sooner. I had to find a temporary home until the courthouse roof was repaired."

Auric hung his head in shame. "I'm the one who should ask to be forgiven. Jealousy and false pride caused me to reject your thoughtful gift. I hope you will forget my selfish behavior so we can be friends again."

Fleetwing gladly forgave Auric and they have remained loyal friends ever since. Some day, if you should happen to visit Sunnydale, you will see them together at the top of the clock tower, high over the roof of the courthouse.

# To Brittany's Eyes

PATRICIA LAWTON

Heart-shaped innocence
Plays host to their existence;
Darkening pools from soft brown to black,
Drawing in the truth to questions asked,
Trusting, seeking knowledge
From generations past.

## SHERRY BENIC

# August

A ugust. So hot, so humid, everything sticks. Walking feels more like wading in this heavy air. The road in front of the house is blacktop.

Even so, dust clings to everything. Everywhere else is green and lush, summer at its zenith, trees fully leafed, flowers fully bloomed, and for the children, a sense that time is fully stopped, hanging in the air.

But it is morning, and the heat has not yet stilled their thirst for adventure. Through the haze, the end of the road beckons.

"Mom, can we have a picnic lunch?"

"I guess so. What do you have planned?"

"We're going to ride our bikes to the end of the road. We're going to watch the planes."

Peanut butter and jelly sandwiches wrapped in waxed paper are dropped into brown paper bags. Apples. School thermoses filled with Kool-Aid. Potato chips. Mom packs a mean picnic.

Sugarbush Road has been there a long time. It twists and curves, winding round small farms and past Green School, over the creek and alongside Mr. Trinity's Library, eventually into New Baltimore.

Today though, when tennis shoes meet bike pedals, the children turn the other way; a blue Huffy and a red Schwinn roll down the driveway and turn left onto the old, pot-holed road.

No traffic today. Mid-morning, mid-week, mid-summer, and not many cars have a need to travel down this country road. Across the way, deep in old Mrs. Goike's pasture, cows drowse. Next door, the Goike house is closed up, the Goikes and their five kids away on vacation. Down at the corner, Mrs. Goike's dad pokes at his garden with a hoe. He waves as the children ride by.

Waiting for two cars to pass, they cross 21-Mile-Road to the next leg of Sugarbush. Here, the trees grow close to the edges of the road, their branches sometimes meeting overhead. The sugar beet fields that gave the road its name no longer exist. The air is a little cooler here under this leafy canopy.

The bikes pass the Little Store, windows boarded over now. When they were younger, the children ran here on errands for Mom. Now they pass the house where Stella and her brother Doug live. Their mom is really nice, but they wonder why she doesn't stand up straight. She's always hunched over like a witch. Their dad is kind of scary and mean. As she rides by, the girl thinks of brown beer bottles.

Shirley's house sits in its yard on the right, like an old white hen on its nest. Nothing moves. Somewhere a bird calls out. In the distance a dog barks.

Kathy's house is at the end of a long driveway. Her older brother is big and blonde. Kathy is so quiet and shy it's hard to play with her.

A little farther on they pass Kingsbury Drive, and now the trees thin out and finally end. All around is empty field. Out there, in all that field, is the end of the runway.

The ditch running alongside the road is dry. Here the children drop their bikes and settle into the cushion of the long grass. Cross-legged, they open paper bags whose tops have already begun to disintegrate from the grasps of sweaty hands.

In the distance a jet engine roars to life. Shining eyes focus on the far end of the runway. The jet shimmers in the haze and gathers speed as it moves closer and closer, wheels lifting from the tarmac and folding into its belly, then roaring overhead into the sky.

"That was a C-5!" shouts the boy. He knows them all.

The girl doesn't care. She cringes at the noise, revels in the speed, and takes a bite of her sandwich.

This is how they pass the morning. The boy bounces with the joy of each take-off. Planes fascinate. He dreams of being a jet pilot. She dreams of the places the planes are going.

It is a moment in their lives — a moment of fullness. Later they will stuff the remains of their picnic back into the paper bags. They will ride their bikes back home.

CHARLIE BROUGH

# Trapped Cat

H i, my name is Rat and I have a story to tell you. I am a large striped cat. I weigh about seventeen pounds and live with my family at Ocean Shores, Washington.

One beautiful sunny morning after I had been sleeping on the porch all night, I was going to scratch on the door to wake up my people. But first, I decided to catch me a big fat rodent. They had tunnels going every which-a-way under the dune grass. I figured I could get me one before my people got up. I always like to greet them each morning, and they are as happy to see me as I am to see them.

I was just about to jump on a fat field mouse when a large dog I had never seen before came along and took chase after me. I made a beeline down the road, hoping to outsmart him and make my way home. But the dog was too fast for me, and I had to change plans in a hurry.

I came to a house that had a low woodshed and made a desperate leap, just clearing the jaws of the big dog. Once on top of the woodshed, I was able to leap to the roof of the house.

I never was good at getting down from high places, ever since I was a tiny kitten. As I looked over the situation I spotted a brick thing that seemed to lead down and away from that barking dog. After some deliberation I made my way down the hole — or I should say fell down — only to find it was blocked at the bottom, and full of black sooty powder.

"God of Cats, what do I do now?"

I became a prisoner of the fireplace for what seemed like an eternity before I heard some rattling of the front door of the house.

When the door opened I could hear two ladies' voices, but neither one was a voice I was used to hearing. I felt so afraid. Under such stress, I was afraid to meow. That night I heard them laughing and talking, and figured they wouldn't hurt me. I started to meow so they would find me and help me get out of that would-be tomb.

After a while I heard one voice say, "I think I hear a cat, don't you?"

They listened while I called to them some more. Finally they decided to look for me. I guess there is no reason why they would think a cat would be stuck in the fireplace, so they went to look outside. While they were outside I heard them talking to a man about hearing a cat. He listened and said, "Ya, I hear it all right. There's a crawl space under the house; it's probably there and will come out by itself."

The ladies agreed with him and came back into the house. Soon after, they went to the other end of the house and must have gone to bed. I was very tired myself. I had been hunting most of the previous night and was very sleepy, so I put my paw over my nose to keep out the black soot and caught a couple zees myself.

The next morning the ladies got up and scurried around the house for a while. As far as I could tell they were packing up to leave. I cried some more, but they didn't hear me, or figured I was still under the house.

With daylight, I tried to see what was below me, but all I could see was more soot and ashes. It wasn't long before the voices got farther away and I heard the front door shut. Then all was quiet. I heard the car start and drive away, leaving me to myself in my silent and sooty prison.

Sadness overwhelmed me. I cried until I was so weak I finally fell asleep.

I was wakened by a noise from above, but I was afraid to come out into the opening. For a while I stayed out of sight. The voice said, "Last night I figured the cat was under the house, but now I'm sure the sound is coming from inside the fireplace."

I recognized the voice as the man I heard the night before. I got to thinking, I better let them see me. If I don't, I'm sure to die down here. The man must be a friend or he wouldn't be trying to get me out.

I moved over so they could see me, and heard another man say, "Hey you're right. There is a cat down there." I could see the man's face looking down at me.

A lady's voice said, "I'll call the police and let them know. Someone must be looking for it."

A little while later the man and the lady were both looking down at me. They talked to me, and after a while the man came back with something tied to a cord. He lowered it down to where I was trapped. It was some sort of a net. I stepped onto it with my paw to see what it was, but just then he started pulling it back up. I should have hung on, but chickened out and let go. Once back in the soot I kicked myself for being such a fraidy cat.

A short time later, a moment I will remember until the dying day of my ninth life, I heard the voice of my Lady. I knew then it was only a matter of time until I would be saved from this sooty grave. The tears rolled down my sooty face. I was so happy and relieved that my owner knew where I was.

Then I heard another voice that turned out to be the police officer. The people who found me had called him. The officer shined something down at me that hurt my eyes. He got a glimpse of me and hollered down to my Lady. "Must be the cat you're looking for, Ma'am. Looks like a sizeable cat."

I remembered then that it had got totally dark two times since I had been down here. During those times of quiet I thought about all the fun times I had in my life — when I was a baby kitten living in Oregon with the daughter of my present owner. I remember they used to talk about it being the place where the wagon trains first brought people and their animals out West. I remembered that my first owner was moving away and gave me over to her mother who lived on an island called Vashon. I remembered all the fun I had there chasing mice, lemmings, and (when I felt brave enough) a rat from down by the pigpen. I don't know why we moved to the ocean, except I liked it. The dunes are full of rodents, so I am happy here as well.

Later everyone left the rooftop and I heard them talking down inside the house where I was trapped. Not long after that my Lady put her hand up where I was and started petting me and said, "Poor kitty, poor Rat, don't worry; we'll get you out soon."

After a while she tried to pull me free of my prison, but I tensed up, making it difficult to be pulled free. I even found myself hanging onto the bars, making it impossible. I finally wised up and relaxed a little. A short time later, with the help of the police officer wiggling the grates and my Lady gently pulling on me, I was free. My Lady and I were both crying. I couldn't believe she was hugging me, as dirty as I was. I could tell that her love for me was very strong.

She thanked everyone for helping her find her kitty and, with her arms hugging me tight, we headed home. The first thing she did was give me a bite to eat and a bowl of milk. After that I had a bath. I hate baths like sin itself, but in this case I didn't argue. I knew it was a must. After the bath as I was being dried with a towel, I heard my Lady say, "It's going to be awhile before you get clean, Rat, but at least you can now lie on the furniture."

Moments later I mewed that I had to go outside. I knew she was afraid to let me go, but she finally consented. I knew I was being watched from the window. I had planned to do my business and go right back in, but once outside I decided to take a short stroll behind the house. It was there that I thought I might do a little hunting before going back inside.

I settled down next to a game crossing, thinking about when I was in that sooty grave. I remembered how my life had flashed by and all the wonderful times I had hunting. Just as I was about to give it up and go inside, a nice fat lemming came sneaking by. I wasted no time in bagging the game. As I was bringing home my catch, I saw the man of the house coming home from golfing. Knowing I had been lost when he left, he dropped his golf clubs and ran to greet me. Both he and my Lady didn't want me eating lemmings and wanted me to drop it. I wouldn't let it go though; I'm a real sportsman and don't like wasting game once I bag it. They think it is best for me to eat moist meals, which is all right, but it doesn't taste like wild game.

It's been four days now; my people are loving the heck out of me. It will be some time before I will be really clean again; my tongue gets so dirty from bathing my sooty hair that I have to stop for a while.

All is well now. Hope I can stay out of trouble. Thanks to all who helped save my life.                                          Rat.

## Jean Hannan

# Jack — The Jack-o-Lantern That Wanted To See Christmas

A family of pumpkins grew from seeds that A.J. planted below the trellis on an outside wall of their house. The pumpkins would not be large, just the right size to become jack-o-lanterns for A.J.'s daughter Kimberly and her friends.

As they grew through the summer, the pumpkins hung around together on the trellis, bobbing hellos to Kimberly and swaying to the rhythm of the backyard swing. The pumpkin leaves rustled in the breeze.

Time passed — summer became fall. Their lives changed. Her mother A.J. talked about which of the pumpkins Kimberly would choose for her jack-o-lantern and which they would give to other children.

The one Kimberly chose became a grinner, with two sharp teeth and a wide mouth. At night, or even on a dark day, a candle inside the jack-o-lantern lighted up the carved face. From all the names Kimberly and A.J. tried out, Kimberly chose Jack. That was his first name; 0 was his middle name, and Lantern was his last name.

He became a decoration wherever he was sitting — on a table, a shelf, or window ledge. He became part of the family: Kimberly, her mother A.J., her father Kip, and Simon The Cat.

When Halloween came around, Jack was set in a window so he could see grownups and children walking by or those who came to their house. He could wink at trick-or-treaters, big and little, in their costumes. He saw ghosts and witches and clowns and hobos and more. They would call out "Trick or treat" and Kimberly would give each one candy or a cookie. Jack loved the excitement of the first holiday he had ever seen.

Jack was sorry that Halloween was over and gone. Was that why he felt much older? His smooth, plump face with the cheery grin had a worried look, more worried every day. He felt alone, except for Simon The Cat.

Simon was furry white. He had spent the summer lolling in the garden under bushes. Now he lay sleeping most of the days inside the house. He didn't pay attention to Jack. Jack wished Simon would talk to him so there would be something going on.

Soon Jack began hearing talk of Thanksgiving. He wondered: What is that? What is Thanksgiving? Kimberly came home from school with pictures of Pilgrims and Indians and turkeys and other pumpkins. Jack wondered if he would be part of the family for this holiday too. He listened to find out more. Thanksgiving, he thought, must be important if it has its own special day.

Even before Thanksgiving came, Jack's little family began to talk about Christmas. Christmas — what could that be? So much to learn here. Christmas sounded like more fun than Thanksgiving. Jack made a wish: I want to see Christmas.

But first there was Thanksgiving. More of Kimberly's family came for dinner. It was a special dinner with turkey and cranberries, just as the Pilgrims had shared with the Indians 400 years ago. There was pumpkin pie. Pumpkin? Jack wondered if it was anyone he knew. There was mince pie. And oyster stew for supper before the family went home.

Before they said their thanks and good-byes, A.J. brought out a basket filled with names of everyone in the family. Each one drew the name of someone to be given a gift at Christmas. Jack said to himself, "I hope I can be here for Christmas."

Thanksgiving was over. Pictures of Pilgrims and turkeys disappeared. Jack had nothing to do but watch for signs of Christmas.

He knew that Simon The Cat could move about the house as he wished. He could even pop through the special little door cut just for Simon, and there he would be — outdoors.

Jack just sat, and only where someone placed him. Sometimes he was lucky to be in the right place. When A.J. and Kimberly made cookies, Jack was on the counter to watch. But when they needed more room for frosting and decorating cookies, A.J. moved him to a bookshelf in the living room. Lucky Jack — he could see more there. Everyone came and went in and out, and Jack could listen and watch.

But Jack was worried. When A.J. had carried him into the living room, he saw himself in the mirror over the fireplace. He saw wrinkles. He knew he was getting old. Would he last until Christmas?

There were signs of Christmas. A.J. brought boxes and boxes in from storage. She took out tinsel to decorate windows, and green and red colored balls for the fireplace mantel. The little stuffed dolls she had made filled baskets to sit on shelves.

Jack could still not guess what Christmas was about. Simon The Cat had been no help at all, telling Jack, "You'll know it when you see it."

One day Kimberly's grandmother, Jeanne-mere, came to visit bringing brightly wrapped packages and gifts in bags. That was the day the green tree was brought into the living room. While A.J. and Kimberly decorated the fragrant fir branches, Jeanne-mere discovered Jack sitting on the bookshelf. "What's this? A jack-o-lantern in December?"

A.J. explained "That's Jack-O-Lantern. You remember him. He is the jack-o-lantern who wants to see Christmas."

"Do you think he will last until then?" She looked at Jack's wrinkled face, his shrunken teeth, and the burned out candle. "Let's help him as much as we can. We'll draw pictures of him and take pictures of him. He is very special."

They set Jack up on the picnic table in the backyard where they could sketch and snap pictures. Now Jack knew he had to last until Christmas.

When Jack was carried back into the living room, he saw something else new to him — the green cotton string wall hanging in the shape of a flat, green tree.

"Yes," A.J. offered, as if she knew Jack would be wondering, "Jeanne-mere brought that to us from South America. We hang it on our wall every Christmas season."

Each day Jack watched from the bookshelf. The fir tree was decorated with colored glass balls, more tinsel, with toys and small stuffed animals. Finally the star was hung from the very top of the tree. The Star of Bethlehem shone down on the room, the bookshelf where Jack sat, and onto the many packages scattered on the red felt under the tree. Jack had learned a new word: festive.

The house smelled of fresh fir boughs and freshly baked Christmas bread. A fat cookie jar, filled to its lid, was ready for guests. With so much excitement going on around him, Jack's face looked less worried and smilier. He liked the holiday music playing softly in the background. All this was worth wishing for and living for!

That evening Jack's little family put on their most colorful coats and, as they were going out the door, A.J said to Jack, "We're going to the Christmas program at church. There will be singing and children and grownups in bright costumes for the play about Christmas." Jack knew he would be lonely, but he was glad the music was playing in the background.

At last, after weeks of waiting, it was Christmas Eve. Neighbors came by for a cheery hello and cookies. Jack heard A.J. say, "Santa Claus is coming — tonight!" Before Kimberly went to bed she set out a plate of cookies for Santa.

The busy day had made Jack so tired that he dozed and never did see or hear Santa. But when he awoke Christmas morning, the cookies were gone and there were more toys and gifts under the tree.

Such excitement — greetings and hugs and such happiness Jack had never seen. Not on Halloween. Not on Thanksgiving. This was different. Jack felt that he too had received the gift of Christmas.

He had been afraid he would not live long enough to see Christmas. But he had! Jack the Jack-O-Lantern was celebrating Christmas!

GALE TRUETT RICHARDSON

# Serenity, Courage And Wisdom

*God grant me the serenity to accept*
*The things I cannot change,*
*The courage to change the things I can,*
*And the wisdom to know the difference.*

S erenity raced in through the front door. "We've got to do something!" she shouted. Her twelve-year old sister, Wisdom, tilted her head slightly and waited. She knew Serenity would tumble out the story.

"The eggs hatched! The eggs hatched!" the child cried out.

Wisdom patted her shoulder like the four-year-old her sister was. "Calm down," she said, wishing Serenity was more like her name indicated. "Chicken eggs hatch every day."

"Don't you understand?" Serenity pouted. "Mother Hen wanted to be a mom, but we didn't have a rooster to fertilize her eggs. So we gave her duck eggs instead. They hatched! The ducks are swimming in the lake!" Serenity wiped the sweat off her brow and stuck her bottom lip out.

Wisdom scratched her head. "So? Ducks always swim."

Serenity sighed loudly, her shoulders lifting then falling. She let out another long sigh, then said, "Chickens don't know that. Mother Hen tried swimming to save them and Courage went in after her."

"He can't swim either," Wisdom said, trotting out the door to rescue her five-year-old brother. Once in the open, she broke into a full gallop.

"I know," Serenity grumbled, pushing her short legs in an effort to keep up with her sister.

When Wisdom got to the lake, it was all she could do not to laugh at her brother's head bobbing just above the water. Mother Hen sat on top of his head, clutching his hair and clucking in fright. The ducklings swam excitedly around them as if to ask their mother, "What's the matter?"

Wisdom carried Courage and Mother Hen to shore. "Why did you do that?" she teased her brother. "You know you can't swim."

Courage scrambled out of Wisdom's arms. "I did swim," he insisted.

"You weren't swimming. You were standing on your tiptoes. Any farther and you would have drowned," Wisdom scolded. Her mom had told her she had to sound gruff or Courage would never learn to ask for help.

Carefully she set Mother Hen on the ground. After shaking herself dry, Mother Hen raced back to the water's edge. This time she stopped. Then she paced along the shore, back and forth, calling again and again to her little ones.

Serenity giggled. "Mother Hen learned she can't swim," she said. Wisdom nodded and silently began to gather twigs with vines.

Finally, curiosity won over shame and Courage asked softly, "What are you making?"

Wisdom kept her eyes on her work. "A boat for Mother Hen."

"Oh, goody! Can I take her out to her babies?" Serenity asked, jumping up and down.

Wisdom looked up and smiled at her. "Of course. You know how to swim. But only if I, Mom or Dad go with you."

Courage looked oddly at his younger sister, then at his older one. He smiled a bashful half-smile. "Wisdom, will you teach me to swim?"

# Duchess
## In Memory of my Siberian Husky
## 1987 - 2001
### P. JUNE DIEHL

She stands magnificent
At the edge of my autumn woods.
Proud
In her wolf heritage,
Beautiful
In her stance and form.

Deep brown eyes
To spot the animal intruders
Invading her land.
A warm coat blankets
Her body,
Out of place in this warmer-than-Husky climate.

Does she await the cold of winter?
The snow of another time?

Always playful,
Even as she approaches her elder years,
A gentle creature,
Caring, loving, and strong.

Howling
At some unheard-by-human sound,
She's wolf and dog,
Crying back to some unknown time.

Gone now,
No more do I hear her howls;
No more do we play;
No more touching that gentle soul.

She stands magnificent
At the edge of heaven's snowy woods.

# Dreamscapes

(Fantasy)

> O, wonderful, wonderful,
> and most wonderful wonderful!
> and yet again wonderful,
> and after that out of all hooping.
> —Shakespeare

# To Dream
## Donna Anderson

To dream is to delve deeply into your soul.
You dare to see things as you know they can be.
You know things that you dare to see.
You see things that you dare to dream.

JANELLE MERAZ HOOPER

# Gets Tickled and the Fish Trap

*Downtown Tacoma, the year 2100...*

T he injured war veteran took a crumpled piece of paper out of his pocket and checked the address. This was it: 2121 Pacific. He stepped back and surveyed the shiny black glass that fronted the building. There was no sign above the door. *Who ever heard of a bus station with no sign?*

He shrugged and walked through the door. Instantly, he found himself in a Cross Country Bus Station — a company that had been gone for years. Empty benches for waiting passengers lined one side of the room and a 1950's style luncheonette, complete with chrome stools and plastic counter, was on the other. The waitress smiled at him and motioned for him to sit in the chair nearest the cash register. He noticed that every seat at the counter was filled, but no one was eating. Instead, they all seemed to be waiting for something.

Somehow the young vet felt that he was part of the reason for their wait, although he couldn't imagine why. Another strange thing: all of the other diner patrons were Indians. They smiled as if they knew him.

He heard a rattle from above, then a loud, girlish giggle. Looking up, he saw a huge fish trap woven out of twigs hanging above his head. The waitress said softly as she went past him, "You're next, honey. You take care now."

The Indian next to him cried out in delight when a live salmon fell from the huge basket onto the counter in front of him. There hadn't been any salmon in Puget Sound for years. The grateful man picked up the thrashing fish, put it under his arm, and left. The next Indian moved up to sit in his place.

When the first fish came down, the veteran was sucked up into the trap. Just then, another vet hesitantly came through the door. The waitress smiled at him and motioned for him to sit in the first chair by the cash register.

The Indian next to him smiled and shook his hand. "I am Running Water. And you are Pete."

"How did you know?"

"We've been waiting for you."

"Why am I here? Where am I going?" asked Pete.

"Up there." Running Water looked towards the ceiling.

Just then, there was a rattle above and a huge fish fell in front of the Indian man. At the same time, the vet felt himself being pulled up toward the ceiling. Running Water picked up the fish, put it under his arm, and left. The next Indian moved up. Another vet came through the door and was seated.

Meanwhile, Pete found it slow going as the trap narrowed. He was surprised that he wasn't in pain. At the end, his head bumped against the inside of the lid of an old iron pot-bellied stove. The lid rattled as a young woman named Gets Tickled opened it. With no effort, she pulled Pete through the small hole into her kitchen where he saw a huge pile of live salmon in the corner.

"Who's down there now?" she asked Pete. "Oh, it's Rock's Hard," she answered herself as she peeked through the hole. "He and his wife are alone now." She picked up a smaller fish and threw it down. Rock's Hard waved and called, "Thank you, Gets Tickled." A loud giggle answered him. He picked up his fish and went home.

The veteran who was pulled up the fish trap as Pete came in was still in Gets Tickled's kitchen. Both men felt themselves pulled toward the beach outside Gets Tickled's front door.

"Hi, I'm Pete."

"Good to know you. I'm Charley. Have you noticed your pain has gone? Mine has."

"Yeah. When I first felt myself being pulled toward that contraption downstairs, I was sweatin' it. I've been in constant pain for months and I thought that being pulled up to the ceiling was going to kill me, but I didn't even feel it."

"The flight didn't hurt me either," Charley agreed.

"Check this out," Pete said to Charley as they approached two new lounge chairs. "Lounge chairs with our names printed on them — just like Hollywood."

The two stretched out in the comfortable chairs and felt the

212

warm sun soak into their skin. Their clothing changed into swim-suits.

"There's quite a few of us here," Charley said as he looked around the beach. "Maybe we should go over and introduce ourselves."

"Good idea. Just let me rest here for a little bit first. I want to savor this body that for the first time since the war isn't hurting me anywhere."

Pete fell asleep and Charley watched him softly breathe in and out. While Pete slept, another man appeared. So did a new lounge chair with the name "Frank." Charley shook his hand.

"What the hell am I doing here?" the befuddled man asked. "First I'm getting off a plane in the middle of a desert, the next thing I'm going through some crazy fish basket in a bus station diner."

"Were you on duty there?" Charley asked.

"Hell, no, I was there to pick up the body of my brother, who was killed in the desert war."

"You went over there to pick him up? That's unusual."

"I know, but my mother has some kind of crazy idea that a man's spirit is still alive for days after he dies, and she didn't want my brother to be alone. She begged me to go pick him up."

"Talk about being in the wrong place at the wrong time. You must have been pegged as a soldier like the rest of us."

"How's that?"

"I don't know," Charley admitted. "We're hoping to find out more later."

"Are we dead?"

"We're not alive. I know that because I'm no longer in pain. Are we dead? Don't know. Must be."

"This, whatever it is, is a mistake. I've got to get back. I'm not dead. I'm not even sick."

Charley looked over to see that the whole crowd was moving toward tables laden with food. He was famished. "Let's go eat. Maybe we'll find some answers while we're over there," he said.

Pete opened his eyes, saw the newcomer, and leaned over and shook Frank's hand. Nothing after today would surprise him; he supposed that the newcomer got there the same way he did.

"Pete, this is Frank. We need to see if we can get him back down through that Indian basket. He's here by mistake."

"Frank, you must have a hell of a story. I can't wait to hear it, but let's eat first."

It was a happy group that gathered around the food-laden table. The whole scene was like something out of a '50's beach movie.

Pete asked John, a man beside him, "Where are we anyway?"

"That's a common question around here. The best we can figure, we're in some kind of a holding pattern for veterans. Maybe some kind of a dimension/purgatory kind of thing. None of us really knows." John loaded his plate while he talked.

"How long have you guys been here?" Charley asked.

John shrugged. "It's hard to tell. Maybe minutes. Maybe days. We're not sure if they have time here."

"That's fine for the rest of us, but Frank is here by mistake. How do we get him back on earth?" Charley asked.

"I don't know of anyone who has ever gone back. Frank, can you remember how you got here?"

"I was slightly injured while I was in the desert, but I wasn't a soldier. My brother was killed over there." Frank searched the beach for his brother.

"Is his brother here?" Charley asked John.

"No, you guys are the only new men here."

"Why wouldn't he be here somewhere?" Pete asked. "Aren't we all soldiers?"

"Yes, but if you look around, there's not enough of us to account for all the battle deaths. We think that there's a common thread that brings us all here, but we don't know for sure what it is. For right now, let's try to figure out how to get Frank back home," John suggested.

"Any ideas?" Charley asked.

"There is a girl here who seems to be the hostess. Maybe she'll help us out with Frank. Here she comes now." John lifted his arm and waved over a young woman wearing a swimsuit with a baggy khaki shirt pulled over the top for modesty. "Hey, Lauren, can we talk to you for a minute?"

"Hey guys, what's up? Not enough food?"

"No problem there," the man joked as he surveyed the laden table. "We've got a stowaway here. This is Frank. He's not a soldier. He wasn't even injured."

"Where were you?" Lauren asked Frank.

"I was in the desert to pick up my brother's body. He was the soldier."

"I haven't had a pickup scheduled there today. Do you remember anything?"

214

"I just remember that I picked up a little boy who was crying and helped him find his mother. All of a sudden, I was flying up into some sort of basket. I ended up here."

"I'll see what I can do." Lauren made a note on her clipboard.

"Have you seen my brother?" Frank asked Lauren.

"Frank, if your brother is dead, you'll never see him again. I'm sorry. Only a few wounded vets ever come here."

"What few is that?" Charley broke in to ask.

"Only soldiers who were trying to save someone else's life. We have other levels with soldiers from the other sides of the battle lines. We keep you guys separate so you can get some rest."

"We're dead and we still can't get along?" Charley asked.

"Dead? What makes you think you're dead? You're just moved to a different level, away from your real body, while you either go through difficult surgery or recover from a coma. Didn't you see your medical charts on the backs of your lounge chairs?" Lauren pointed to a pocket in the back of each lounge chair. Turning to Frank she said, "Let me check this out. I'll get back to you."

Sometime during the night Lauren gently shook Frank's shoulder. "Wake up, Frank. You were right. This was a mistake. You're going home."

"That's great. How?"

"I'll take you back. While I'm down there, I have a pickup to make. I have to deliver your little Arab boy to the Mid-Eastern level."

"What did he do?"

"He stepped in front of his mother to protect her from gunfire."

"Sounds like him. When will he be able to go home?"

"He won't. At eight-thirty tomorrow morning the whole Mid-East will be gone. Some maniac will use nuclear weapons and misjudge their power. Israel, Iran, Iraq — all of them — will be contaminated for years."

"Isn't God going to stop it?"

"I don't think so, Frank. From what I hear, He's had it with all of them."

"That's a story to take back home."

"Sorry. You won't remember this conversation or this place when you get back to earth."

Lauren's voice began to fade and Frank heard his wife's voice plead as she shook his arm, "Frank, Frank! Are you okay?"

Frank opened his eyes to find he was stretched out on a sidewalk on Pacific Avenue surrounded by 911 medics. Had it all been a dream?

"Honey, what are you doing in this part of town? We were supposed to pick you up at the airport — and where did you get this big salmon?" his curious wife asked.

Frank looked over and saw a huge salmon flopping around next to him on the sidewalk. "Honey, I swear, I've never seen that fish before in my life," he said.

No one but Frank heard the girlish giggle that floated down between the office buildings. A big smile moved across his face, but he didn't know why.

# NANCY COVERT

# Through the Glass Darkly

*Dateline:* WASHINGTON POST
*Washington DC, June 14, 2002 — Prospects for legislation to ban the cloning of human cells, one of the most contentious issues facing Congress and the White House, dimmed considerably Thursday as negotiations over the ground rules collapsed…*

There was no reason to set the alarm. My well-tuned internal clock would make sure I'd be wide awake without any buzzer ringing — a well-tuned internal clock and about a decade of ingrained habit.

What's that saying: "Old habits die hard"? Ironic, since a habit of a different color started it all.

The airport shuttle was scheduled to pick me up forty-five minutes later for the trip to Sea-Tac Airport. Plenty of time before boarding the red-eye. All because of that face.

The first time I'd seen it was on a movie screen at a Saturday matinee. I was about nine. Years later, after undergoing rigid security checks, I was given access to classified data. The debate about the identity though had continued for more than seven centuries: A crucified Roman? An expendable crusader? Whose image was really on the shroud?

In less than an hour, I'd embark on a pilgrimage that Chaucer's travelers never imagined, without any Nun's Pardoner to lighten the journey. In about a month we'd know.

A bored airport security attendant waved me through the electronic portal. I watched my bag slide through the curtained conveyor.

"I beg your pardon?"

"We see through a glass darkly, but then face to face," the attendant repeated. Bizarre.

The slim passport I'd updated lay at the bottom of the nondescript black leather briefcase I'd been issued. Everything I'd need for the next two weeks was packed inside. "Ta da! The grand entrance," I quipped as I stepped through the scanner.

"Whatever," the baggage checker fidgeted, adjusting her too-tight uniform.

X-rays had started this whole thing, I recalled, replaying a confidential conversation from half a year earlier. Carbon dating tests had proven inconclusive. With advances in cloning techniques, the plan was set in motion. While others were hesitant about "playing God," mission support came from an unlikely quarter.

One late October afternoon I was ushered into a lavish Victorian parlor. The room, furnished with fine mahogany settees and claret-colored velvet cushions, seemed more appropriate for a Regency novel. By the end of the session, I'd filled my notebook with explicit instructions.

The next morning, I reported to the gym for the first workout.

"More rigorous than SEAL training," the very fit and undoubtedly well-qualified instructor boasted, sounding like Moses delivering The Word. Preparations included outings to the landmark, glacier-cloaked, dormant volcano for timed runs over upper elevation trails.

"You can hold your own against any commando, even a knight," my trainer said before I left at the end of April.

Half an hour after the 747 had landed at Turin's International Airport, I hailed a Fiat cab to deliver me to the small stucco pensione. I'd taken refuge in a convent that supplemented its income by housing tourists — another irony — but a refreshing change from pricey, glitzy city hotels. Located about a mile from the cathedral with its soaring bell tower, the sparsely furnished room's narrow window overlooked a peaceful garden. Late afternoon sunlight cast a creamy rectangle on the bare, well-scrubbed pine floor. The feeling of stepping back in time surrounded me as I unpacked.

The tumblers of the combination lock clicked into place and I opened a hidden compartment. Instruments gleamed jewel-like against the communion wine-red velvet padding. Checking each piece to ensure nothing had been damaged, I resealed the divider.

The two-piece navy blue suit rustled as I removed it from the bag.

A gentle vibration, pulsating from the innocent-looking copper bracelet on my wrist, reminded me that I had yet to make a call. One pay phone, available for the guests' use, was located in the main hallway. I locked the door, glided across the patio to the lobby, and dialed.

"This is V. All is well," I replied to the androgynous voice on the other end.

I spent the rest of the afternoon reviewing plans. The only interruptions were the gentle chiming of the bells, marking the centuries-old rituals: Angelus, Compline, Nones, then nothing.

Except for a vivid dream — fueled no doubt by too much caffeine — populated with fierce, armored soldiers battling equally determined adversaries, the night slipped into day as the convent's resident rooster announced the sun's return.

After a simple breakfast of convent-baked bread, fresh milk, a tangy chevre, and silent prayer, I hiked into the city to join the throng of pilgrims queued outside the 600-year-old church of San Giovanni Bautista. In the past six months the reports of miracles had increased, attracting more visitors to the sacred site.

"The city has enough of interest to justify a one-night stay, but no more," the stateside travel agent had advised. Fine with me. A day was all I needed.

A heavy fog of incense descended as I stepped over the threshold into the basilica. Inching forward with the throng of weeping, sighing, dark-clothed believers, I followed the signs to the chapel. Although I'd practiced the routine so many times in the Chapter House, this was my first view of the actual building. The target lay ahead on an ornate, high Renaissance altar. Last put on public view on the four hundredth anniversary of its acquisition, the sacred cloth was now stored out of sight.

It was well protected: inside an elaborate silver casket; in turn housed inside an iron box, a marble coffin and a heavy urn. I had to give them credit. They'd done a good job. The rest was up to me. As I passed the relic, I genuflected, lit a votive, scoped out a good spot for my midnight vigil, then exited the church. The noonday heat was a marked contrast to the cathedral's dark coolness.

I returned to the church later that afternoon, slipping unobserved inside the sanctuary. A musty smelling, out-of-the-way confessional I'd spotted earlier was to be my base. The combination of darkness and clammy chill were tolerable. Another image, one from an early scene in Puccini's tragedy, Tosca, came to mind as I waited. I adjusted the wrist alarm, rechecked the instruments in the leather fanny pack beneath my dark blue sweatshirt, then made myself comfortable on the confessional's bench. Resting on the dusty cushion, I let my mind wander while my body slumbered.

I watched bigger-than-life images fill the space: thundering destriers, heavily armored knights, shattering lances, then blood, blood and more blood as crusading invaders clashed with natives. My displaced spirit watched as a heavily cloaked and hooded man offered up a bundle of fabric to an exhausted knight. Even as I slept, I understood that my rational brain was on overload. Too many tales about Knights Templar and Geoffrey de Charney's role in this mad escapade.

The wrist alarm awoke me as the last of the church bells reverberated through the building. Their funereal sound resonated like aftershocks of a six-point-eight earthquake.

Alert for any sound, I stretched to jumpstart my circulation. Flickering votives multiplied my shadow, morphing this party of one, ala Catherine Zeta-Jones, into a group of elongated, El Greco-style shapes. I fumbled with the fanny pack's zipper, removed an energy bar, peeled it, and bit off a chunk, stashing the remainder.

Using the damp stone wall for support — moral and physical — I inched forward. I tried to blend into the background as I approached the relic that beaconed from the high cloth-draped altar. Despite its protective layers, the hidden face challenged me. Long-dead eyes bore through me. I shivered.

"Just a goose walking over my grave," I muttered, swiping at the sheen of sweat on my brow. Moisture itched beneath the tight black hood I had donned. Unfastening a laser from my tool belt, I proceeded.

Faint clinks were the only indication that the protective layers had been breached. I paused. A faint rustling. Silence. I removed the first vial from the pack; my fingers trembled as they touched the cloth inside the final container. After thirty excruciatingly long minutes, the first part of the mission was complete. Stepping back from the altar I made sure there was no trace of my witching hour visit. I crossed myself and returned to the confessional sanctuary.

Too easy" was the thought uppermost in my mind. But I was easily distracted by the steady, but not very effective, sweep of windshield wipers against the thick gray mist that swirled outside. I didn't give it much thought. Driving on the wrong side was enough of a challenge, especially along this windy highland road. Haunting melodies of Hildegard von Bingen's soulful music filled the car as I watched for stray lambs. I rechecked the map and, for reassurance, patted the bulky bag stored on the passenger seat. In the dim early morning light, I could barely make out the contents' outline.

Steering carefully around a sharp bend in the road, I caught sight of the institute. I'd expected to find a brooding concrete structure with barbed wire. Instead, the scene before me looked like something you'd see on a vacation postcard. Wish you were here. Although with what was to come, some wit might have scribbled a comment on the back about unholy experiments.

A modest bronze plaque, announcing the "de Charney Research Institute," was centered on the gate. My foot tapped the brakes. A red-haired attendant, attired in a crisp white uniform bearing a white shield and red cross logo, waved me through the checkpoint after verifying my credentials.

"You're expected," she said, her rich brogue washing over me like the first sweet stinging sip of Drambuie. Charming, but I'd also noticed her sidearm. I returned the salute, a poor imitation of her well-practiced snap.

A choir of white-coated techies watched as I parked the grey Land Rover. Then, I handed over the bag.

"Well done! You've earned a rest."

I nodded and followed another techie, who ascended a curving flight of stairs to an inviting, warm, third floor room.

"Might as well relax. It will be awhile before we have any results."

Fine with me. I tossed my bags in a corner, removed my shoes, plumped up the pillows and crashed on the soft, down-filled duvet for a long dreamless sleep, a sweet scent of incense my last sensory impression. It had been too easy. But then, it had been a distaff operation.

A toast to your efforts," said the austere older woman sitting across from me later that afternoon as we gathered beside a crackling fire. Five women raised their teacups in salute.

"Beatrice should begin writing the results by the end of the week," the older woman continued.

"So soon?" another asked.

"The breakthrough in cloning has been remarkable,..." our

hostess replied, "…almost bordering on the miraculous. With just the small sample Veronica was able to get — quite successfully, I might add — we will finally have an answer. It was truly provident when you joined our Order." She nodded at me.

I acknowledged her praise with mixed emotions. After I'd left Special Forces for this higher calling, it seemed as though every assignment I received had directed me toward this moment.

"Hurry!" an agitated-looking technician beckoned from the doorway. Seven porcelain teacups clattered like a small rockslide as we rose in unison and followed her to the secure laboratory, three chilly levels underground.

Bringing up the rear, I glanced at a collection of Abbesses' portraits lining the oak-paneled walls, their expressions conspiratorial. In the distance I heard a persistent hum, like the sound of beating wings.

As marble statues in a cathedral, the women stood, frozen in place around the worktable.

"Saints preserve us!"

"We'll need more than saintly intervention!"

"Better call the Holy Mother!"

Now we see through a glass darkly, but then face to face.

# Seduction

## GALE TRUETT RICHARDSON

Candlelight soothing my sorrow,
  They come like phantoms in the night,
    Swirling like fireflies in summer,
      Thrilling me with torments and delights.

Summer sun and sweet smelling grasses,
  Perfumes that rise to inspire,
    They circle and hug and entice me
      Beyond my wildest desire.

Caresses of velvet and jasmine
  In moonlight as pale as ghosts,
    Lingering gently above me,
      Silent, solitary hosts.

Offering a smorgasbord of enticement
  They play many scenes in my mind,
    Of the future that lures me forward
      And the past I can't leave behind.

Memories and hopes on their wing tips,
  The haunts of Ireland's blarney stone,
    Steering me into strange musings
      Of ancient lands I once roamed.

Casually they sit beside me
  In St. Patrick's Church, McDonalds or McGees,
    Fluttering their suggestive longings,
      Ideas getting the best of me.

So I sit down at the computer
  And give life to their dreams and mine,
    Co-creators in a vast reality
      Of all the words I can find.

## SHERRY BENIC

# The Healing

*S*he sat near the fire for warmth, its flickering light casting shadows on the fabric in her hands. The needle flashed in and out...in and out...her lips moved in a silent litany.

Lilah was cold. Rain slopped down around her, mud squelching up through the straps of her sandals. She shivered and pulled her jacket tighter. It was no use. The jacket was soaked, her hair a sodden and tangled mass. The rain had long ago washed away every trace of makeup; now it mingled with the tears on her cheeks. She wiped at her runny nose with the back of her hand.

One foot moved in front of the other. All around her the night was dark and cold and wet.

*My creation, she thought. Mine, for her. In her mind she saw the figure wrapped in the cloth, standing tall, strong, fierce. The feeble glow of the dying embers flashed from the needle as it moved in and out.*

Fingers numb, lips blue, legs scratched and cut by the brambles she had stumbled through — cuts washed clean by the freezing rain — she put one foot in front of the other. Night of the Living Dead. I am the Living Dead. The thought leaped from the numb jumble in her mind. I am a zombie, I guess. Am I dead? Is this hell? Not hot at all...Left foot. Right foot. Left foot. I can't feel my toes.

*Her lips moved, forming silent words. Wrap her in your love, Lord Jesus. Warm her. Protect her. Keep her safe and strong, Lord Jesus. Outside the wind howled, a shutter banged...while inside the needle flashed.*

She didn't know where she was, hadn't known since she had run into the cold and wet, away from...that.

There was no moon to show her the way, no stars; there was only a black midnight of rain. Rain. And cold. It's so cold. So very cold. I want to go home. Please, God, let me go home where I can be safe, where I can be warm.

Left foot. Right foot. Bony fingers snatched at her hair, scraped her cheeks — no, just branches. Was he behind her? Following? He'd been cursing, violently angry, trying to rock the car out of the rut. Forward and back, jamming the gears from drive to reverse while the tires spun. Already dazed, she felt again the pressure of his hand against her throat, could hear the fabric of her blouse ripping…a primal reaction…fight or flight…. As he threw the car again into reverse and gunned the engine, she yanked open the door and stumbled into the dark.

*Softly she began to hum the old words, "…there is a balm in Gilead. Let this shawl be blessed as a balm, Lord Jesus, that when she put it round her she feel warm and strong and safe, and she know…she know…she gon' be okay…. Guide her to the safety of this creation."*

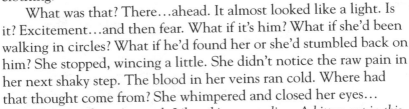

She couldn't run any more. The stitch in her side hurt something awful. In fact, she was limping now, her ankle throbbing, but she didn't remember hurting it. Didn't remember much, in fact, except the violence beneath his whispers, the snarl on his face as he ripped at her clothing.

What was that? There…ahead. It almost looked like a light. Is it? Excitement…and then fear. What if it's him? What if she'd been walking in circles? What if he'd found her or she'd stumbled back on him? She stopped, wincing a little. She didn't notice the raw pain in her next shaky step. The blood in her veins ran cold. Where had that thought come from? She whimpered and closed her eyes…

*What was that? A sound. Like a kitten mewling. A kitten out in this storm? The woman bundled the cloth into the basket next to her and heaved her bulk from the old rocker. I don' know if my knees or the rocker creaks worse, she thought.*

*Opening the door, she frowned into the dark. Nothing. Wait…there it was again. She moved a few feet into the soggy darkness, nearly stumbling over the pile of rags. No, not rags. Something more solid. A body.*

Lilah looked around the small room, wondering where she was. Flowered wallpaper; and along the wall a basin and ewer on a stand near a chest. Filmy lace curtains across the window. A dim, gloomy light beyond the curtains. Lilah closed her eyes and slept while shadowy figures moved around her.

When she woke again, the room was lighter. A fire crackled on the hearth, flames dancing as if to celebrate their warmth. Now Lilah noticed a stitched sampler on the wall. The verse would have to wait; she couldn't quite make out the letters. She felt the weight of covers pressing against her body — a wedding ring quilt. Counting the detailed stitches, she wondered about the unknown quilter.

"'Bout time you wake." Lilah's eyes followed the low, mellow voice to the doorway. She was a massive woman, a giant of a woman, tall and solid. Like a tree, Lilah thought. Solid and sturdy and strong like an oak. "You 'bout be needin' nourishment, girl. Let's see can you sit up? I he'p you here. We put some pillows here and prop you up. Thass better." The old woman stood back, looked at her patient, and gave the quilt a twitch to straighten it.

"Here, this he'p keep you warm." The old woman tucked a shawl around Lilah's shoulders. "I don' want you to spill on this quilt. My momma stitched this quilt. Here, I hold the bowl and spoon the soup into you mouth. You ain't strong 'nuff yet." The broth was fragrant with chicken and spices, and Lilah's mouth opened to receive the spoon. Delicious! She felt the warmth of it travel through her body. She opened her mouth again.

"Here, baby. I know you got to use the chamber pot. I he'p you. It okay. Coupla day and you good as new." Strong arms lifted her gently, and for a moment she pressed against that warm breast and felt safe again.

"You feel like my mom," Lilah whispered.

"I know, baby, I know." Tenderly the hands arranged the nightgown and shawl, and tucked the quilt around her. "You go back to sleep now. Shhh."

When Lilah woke again it was dark. The sound of soft snoring came from a corner near the hearth. The old woman sat in the rocker, silhouetted against the glowing embers, her head nodding to the rise and fall of her breaths. At Lilah's side a pressure...that purred as she reached her hand to touch it. She closed her eyes.

"How long have I been here?" Lilah asked the old woman. She reached for the bowl of hot oatmeal. Her eyes closed as she tasted the first spoonful...hot and milky, and flavored with brown sugar.

"Jus' 'bout three days now, baby. You healin' real fast. When I found you outside, you was wet clear through. I didn't know but maybe you was dead, you so cold, but I held the mirror to your lips and see your breath, and I know this baby need Granny's doctorin'." She pressed her lips together and shook her head. "Mmm-mmm. I guess God got a big plan for you, baby girl. He bless my hands, and He heal you."

"What should I call you?"

"You jus' call me Granny, same as ever'one else, baby girl."

"What are you working on?"

"Oh, I jus' be stitchin.' I jus' be creatin'. Sometimes I stitch a quilt, sometimes I stitch a sampler. Sometimes I make a garment. Woman is the bringer of life into this world. Woman is the nurturer of life. I just be creating like woman was meant to create, now I too old to bring babies to this world."

"What is it you say while you stitch? I see your lips move, almost like you are praying."

"Well, I guess maybe I am praying, baby girl. When I am creatin', I am prayin'. I pray God's love into every stitch. I pray the protection of God on the owner of whatever I be makin'."

"How do you know who will wear it?"

"Bless you, baby girl. I don't know who will wear it or use it or cover up with it. I just pray for whoever might."

"But why?"

"Because, like I already told you, it my job to create and nurture. You and me, we woman. We bring life to this world. We protect it.

"You be ready to leave here soon," she said, changing the subject. "I seen to your clothes. Washed 'em and pressed 'em. You git back to sleep now. You got a bit of walkin' to do in the morning."

An old green Cadillac pulled up to the gas pumps just as Lilah reached the station. The old man who got out smiled and nodded his white head as he fit the pump nozzle into the Caddie. Lilah smiled back. The morning air felt so good — fresh and clean and invigorating. Funny dream she'd had, though. The old lady and the ancient house with its crackling fire…it sure had been vivid. On a whim, she turned back to the elderly gent. "Can you tell me if there's a bus comes by here? I need to get back to the university."

"Why, shore is. Comes right here. You wait — it'll be by 'bout 11:30. Take you straight on to the college. Mighty pretty shawl you wearin'."

228

Lilah glanced down. Instead of the denim jacket she remembered, she saw soft folds of creamy material. This is the shawl in my dream, she thought. What's going on here?

"Mother!" the old man called out, and a tiny, white-haired lady opened the passenger door of the Caddie.

"Yes, Mr. Clay?"

"Mother, look at this here pretty shawl. Don't that look familiar?"

"Why, that looks like Granny Bell's work. Emmy Lou, her granddaughter, has one nearly like it. Where'd you get that shawl, honey?"

Colors seemed to spin around Lilah...faster and faster until she found the old man gently lowering her onto a bench. His wife handed her a bottled Coke, lines of concern etched between her brows. The world shifted back into focus.

"Why'n't you tell us 'bout it, honey? Might be we could understand."

Slowly, stammering, Lilah repeated the story of her date with Jack, his anger when she refused his demands, and her flight into the rainy darkness. "And then I dreamed I was in an old house with a warm fire. There was a wedding ring quilt on the bed. And a lady. A big, gentle lady who called herself Granny. In my dream, she took care of me, nursed me, and wrapped this shawl around me. She said it would heal me."

The old couple nodded together. "It ain't the first time. Granny Bell was a gifted healer. Folks brought their sick young ones to her. People said nobody could heal like Granny Bell. And she always claimed it wasn't her at all, that the Lord was just using her hands."

"But you said *was*. Where is she now?"

"Child, she been dead a hundred years. Her old cabin's still almost standing out there in the woods; all overgrown now, and fallin' in on itself. Maybe you saw it while you was wandering?"

Goose pimples popped out on Lilah's arms and she shivered. "But what about the shawl? Where did that come from?"

"Folks say she was a wonder with a needle. Say she stitched healing right into the things she made. Might be she made it for you."

## J. R. CARLSEN

# Clock Shop

Falling snowflakes brightened the tiny street, causing dusk to appear like midday, as Richard closed his clock repair shop that Christmas Eve. Last minute shoppers were completing their holiday errands before racing home to their families, but Richard had no one preparing holiday festivities for him.

He was virtually alone in the world since Maria, his wife of twenty years, passed away in her sleep last January. The doctor said her heart was weakened from childhood illnesses from which she never fully recovered. Each recurrence weakened her more until that cold wintry day when she didn't wake from an afternoon nap.

Eleven months after Maria's death, it was understandable that Richard still missed her. Neither Richard nor Maria had siblings, and despite years of trying, they never had any children. All they had were each other and the clock shop. Business slowed over the years, especially when quartz revolutionized the clock  industry. Rarely did anyone require a clock repaired now, as it was cheaper to replace a watch than to repair it. Watch repairs were mainly changing batteries, so most of his business consisted of selling new timepieces rather than repairing existing ones.

A few years earlier, Richard considered branching out his business to include computer repairs, but soon discovered that the computer industry had already surpassed him and was for a younger generation to promote. He did find them interesting and, with Maria gone, his evenings were filled with researching on the Internet. The World Wide Web provided a universe of information, and each evening he discovered a new galaxy of knowledge to explore. His latest discovery was…time travel.

It's not surprising for someone in the clock business to be interested in time, but time travel? Richard's fascination with time travel began as a boy with Orson Wells' story, "The Time Machine." He always felt that one day it would be possible to travel through time, and as he entered adulthood, his certainty grew. Over those years he had read numerous books and had seen every movie made about the subject. Silly movies like "Time Bandits" and the "Back To The Future" trilogy, romantic ones like "Somewhere In Time," and the sci-fi series "Star Trek," along with all the off-shoots, did more than just entertain him. All of them cemented his belief that one day it would happen, a belief which caused him to research the topic on the Internet. Who would expect someone could stumble upon a Web site so simple as www.timetravel.com?

Furthermore, who would have guessed he could actually travel through time just by visiting the Web site using a cable modem operating at a speed of ten megabytes per second via fiber optics? Fact Time or Fantasy Time was the first option Richard found. Thus far, he'd only searched a couple time periods in history, such as the Civil War years to see Abraham Lincoln. He hadn't actually traveled anywhere yet.

A person would have to be very careful in time traveling so they wouldn't interrupt the time continuum established in history. To do that could prove disastrous because it could alter history by actually preventing the future from happening. An interaction not accounted for in history could do that — too scary to even think about. Because of his fear of altering history, Richard decided to travel to Fantasy Time that night, his first trip into time! After all, even if he altered Fantasy Time, how could that affect history? So, who better to visit on Christmas Eve than Santa Claus?

Richard couldn't wait to log onto the Internet and click onto his favorite Web site. With his state-of-the-art computer connections, it was instantaneous for him to be searching Fantasy Time for Santa Claus. He was in such a hurry, he didn't bother to scroll down and read the Caution and Disclaimer Statements at the bottom of the Web site. He'd already read them in the Fact Time section. He had read how actual interaction with people from the past could affect the future, our present. But since he was in Fantasy Time, he didn't think that mattered.

Before he clicked on the Travel button, which would land him in the North Pole, he needed to put on his boots, coat, hat, and scarf. He stuffed his wool gloves in his coat pockets because he couldn't type on the keyboard if he wore them. Then he pointed his cursor on the Travel button and clicked the mouse...

The next sensation Richard felt was how very cold he was. Brrrrr, he thought, I really do need to put those gloves on. It wasn't until he heard the crunch, crunch of the crispy white snow under his boots as he stamped his feet to get warm that he realized he was outdoors — outdoors in an area he'd never seen before and which he presumed was the North Pole. At least that's what the sign read about fifty feet away. "You are now entering the North Pole," he read. "Welcome!"

Richard looked up the winding path to the house on the hill about a half mile away. Could it be...could it really be Santa's house? He approached the snow-covered house cautiously and peered in the window. "Ahhhh!" he exclaimed, thinking how Maria would have enjoyed seeing how festively decorated the inside of this home was. She had always enjoyed decorating their little house for the holidays even though there were only the two of them to enjoy it.

This house had garlands and colorful Christmas lights everywhere. A tree was decorated in the center of the hallway with bright lights and popcorn strung with cranberries. As he pressed his nose against the windowpane he could smell the freshly baked gingerbread, and his mind filled with thoughts of previous Christmases.

It was at this moment that someone entered the room where Richard was looking. It was a man with snow-white hair wearing bright red pants, black boots and a red plaid flannel shirt. "It's him," said Richard aloud, and he felt a quick tap in the middle of his back. He turned around to discover there was a tiny man in a long green stocking-cap standing behind him.

"What are you looking at?" asked the little man. "Why are you spying on Santa?"

"I'm not spying," said Richard. "I've just arrived and I was making sure where I was."

"Arrived?" the dwarf man asked, puzzled, "arrived from where?"

"Canada," said Richard. "I came to meet Santa."

"But, how did you get here? I've been following you for the last half-mile and you just appeared out of nowhere because that's where your tracks begin," continued the man in the green hat. "Come with me! Santa won't be happy about this at all."

The elf led Richard inside, then left him with Santa as soon as he introduced them. After hearing how Richard arrived, a disturbed Santa voiced his thoughts. "I knew that Web site was going to be a problem. We're going to have to do something about that in the time we have left."

"Time...we have left," Richard repeated. "What do you mean?"

"What I mean..." answered Santa, "...is that you have upset the time continuum by coming here. Fantasy time will no longer be the same; it's going to change again, and we have until midnight to make adjustments or Christmas as we know it will end. Oh why did you have to pick the busiest day of the season to decide to time travel here? Never mind, I guess that's obvious!"

Richard, still confused, was about to ask more questions when in walked a white-haired woman wearing a red dress and a white apron and carrying a tray with steaming mugs of hot chocolate and a plate of freshly baked ginger cookies. She looked somewhat familiar, but it wasn't until he heard her voice saying, "I heard we had a visitor and thought you'd enjoy a snack," that he knew.

"Maria!" a startled Richard exclaimed. "Am I dreaming?"

"Oh Richard, I didn't know you were the visitor."

During the next twenty minutes, Santa explained how Maria had joined them from her last dream eleven months earlier. She, too, had come close to altering the time continuum, but since he desperately needed a housekeeper and her tired heart had stopped beating, she stayed on. "Dreams don't normally upset the time continuum, but dying prevents the dream from completing its normal progression," Santa explained.

"That happened after the busy Christmas season, so we had time to think up a solution," Santa continued. "Your time travel visit allows us less than six hours before I'll disappear, and we have all those presents to deliver around the world before then."

"Disappear?" Richard and Maria screamed together.

"Yes, of course," Santa patiently explained. "Richard's talking with me will cause me to disappear. Unlike Maria's arrival via her dream, Richard's interaction with me has changed the course of fantasy history. Now that we have met, I will fade away when the day ends. Richard, you will have to take my place and we have less than six hours to train you."

The rest of the evening was spent going over the details of Santa's last ride, so there was no time for Maria and Richard to converse. She mouthed, "I've missed you!" as Richard and Santa took off with all the presents packed.

They returned at eleven forty-five to find the house dark with sleep, although the fireplace still glowed warmly. Santa moved to the grandfather clock in the corner. He opened the door and stopped the pendulum for a moment as he reached behind it into a secret hiding place. He brought out a large thick envelope and handed it to Richard to open. It began, "Dear Richard," and when Richard looked surprised, Santa replied, "Yes, I knew you were coming! This will explain everything to you that I suspected I wouldn't have time to tell you. I wrote it many, many years ago on the day you were born. You see Richard, this has always been your destiny. Do you remember the year you received Orson Wells' book, "The Time Machine," in your Christmas stocking? It was never on your Christmas list, but I had to plant the seed of time travel somehow."

Those last minutes before midnight passed all too quickly and, as the grandfather clock chimed the last hour, Santa and Richard looked at each other in the mirror over the mantle. Richard watched his hair begin to whiten at a very rapid rate and Santa's image begin to fade. When Richard turned to look at him, he was gone and Richard was now wearing the traditional red suit.

While walking his dog on Christmas morning, Tim noticed lights on in the Clock Shop. He thought this strange since he knew Richard was very thrifty and always turned the lights out when he went home at night. Thinking he must have come in early for something, Tim peered through the window, wanting to wish him a Merry Christmas. He saw someone slumped over the computer in the back room. Worried about Richard, he called 9-1-1.

When the paramedics arrived, they found Richard still in his boots, coat, hat and scarf, lying across his keyboard as if he'd fallen asleep. They couldn't revive him. As the paramedics were taking him away, Tim went to turn off the computer. The search window said: www.timetravel.com, but a message appeared on the screen that read, "Web site no longer available." After shutting off the computer and the lights, he locked the door for the last time and paused to read the gold leaf sign on the window:

The Clock Shop
Richard Nicholas, Proprietor.

KIM RYAN

# Just Around the Bend

**M**aya eventually wandered away from her parents, grabbing a stolen walk when they pulled off the highway for a break. They were following the coastline and she was tired of looking at trees. She was tired of the heavy silences in the car, and being talked about like she wasn't there.

Something was wrong, she could tell, although she was used to the tense worried glances and the hushed speculation that they thought she missed. This time it was more. Something in her mother's silence and her father's strained constant conversation told her that this road trip was no joy ride.

The most they'd told her about where they were going was to a meeting with yet another "wonderful" head doctor they were just sure she was going to love. Maya knew there was more to it than that, and she doubted very much that she'd love any of it. She didn't know what to expect except more of the same: carefully concerned probing questions and clueless diagnosis, during which she would give up nothing, and divide her attention between the clock and the window.

What they hadn't told her, the thing that had her mother staring unseeing at the floor for miles, was that they were planning to leave her behind in residential treatment until she was supposedly back "in touch with reality." They were tired, and weren't going to come up with the nerve to tell her about it until they had to. They loved avoidance and denial, did their best to live by it, and had it down to an art form these days.

They pulled off into a small parking lot and looked down at the beach. As nobody seemed in a hurry to move, Maya got out first, piling through the unread comic books and the fast food wrappers, then leading the way down the path cut through red rock. Her parents followed behind, her father hovering nervously.

"Maya, honey, watch your step, okay? Just slow down a little bit; the rocks are sharp."

"She's okay." It seemed like a vast effort for her mother to speak, and her father didn't respond. They continued along the edge of the water in silence.

It was sunset, Maya's favorite time of day, that time of light when everything glows a peculiar golden pink, showing off what must be the colors of another softer world.

When her parents stopped to stretch out on the still warm sand, Maya stayed standing, trying to edge away from them without appearing to move. She was enchanted with the smell of the sea air, with her bare feet in the sand, with the endless horizon. But of course they noticed when she got a little bolder, walking a short way down the beach.

"Maya, come back this way," her mother called, starting to get up.

"Just let her walk a little, it's all right." Her father kept trying to be soothing and upbeat at the same time, managing only the thinnest appearance of either. Maya kept moving, always alert to opportunity. She could hear them carrying on, but she kept going and they didn't stop her.

Maya decided that she would go exactly as far as she pleased, and then turn around. She wandered at the edge of the water, weaving in and out, following a curve in the beach until she couldn't see her parents anymore. There was no one else around, no one else in the whole world. She investigated the tide pools thoroughly, and climbed over the red-brown rocks when they reached across her path into the sea.

Sometimes the rocks came together and formed caves, which she loved. It was cool inside them, and so dark and sweetly secret. She thought of dragons, fairies, ogres and trolls. Looking at the caves made her think of the magic she knew must be in there. She knew how all those "wonderful" doctors would shake their heads and peer over their glasses and look gently concerned if she, for once even, told them what she knew. Didn't matter. Never mind now. Someday they would understand.

Maya crawled into one of the caves, took a turn, and saw light ahead. A tunnel after all! She'd found a tunnel. She kept going and emerged at a point where an especially tall sheer wall of rock reached out to the water, leaving only the narrowest strip of glowing sand disappearing into the tide. Naturally she had to get around it, see what was around the bend.

Good one, around the bend. The grownups had told her she already was.

As soon as she turned the corner, she saw her — what looked like a naked woman sitting at the edge of a pool in an inlet. Maya stopped, staring. The woman hadn't looked up at her, or reacted to her presence at all, appearing mesmerized by the pink sparkle on the waves. Still Maya felt like she shouldn't be there. She started to back away, feeling vaguely guilty.

The woman's hair was quite long, revealing one perfect breast and falling on into the water below her waistline; she was beautiful in a hypnotic, almost obsessive way. Maya could not have looked away if she had wanted to. She managed to keep backing up while feeling pulled forward, all at the same time.

Then she noticed the flashing silver of diamond scales, waving slowly just underwater. Back and forth the huge tail waved, stirring the fronds that grew in the pool in languid, dreamy motions. The sounds of the small splashes and eddies she made were the songs of other worlds in Maya's mind. Tears fell unnoticed as she listened to the words of verses no one else had ever heard, their message answering all the questions that were inside her, healing all the wounds, making promises that were fulfilled even as they were made.

They stayed that way, looking at each other for immeasurable unmarked time. The air cooled and the shadows deepened, chasing the glowing hues of the sunset underground for another night. Maya knew she was saying goodbye when the mermaid finally slid into the pool, smiling sadly. But then she dove, surfaced again, circled back, appearing to be undecided or unwilling to go. She didn't come back out of the water, but swam there a while longer, apparently torn between the call of the deep sea and the girl on the beach.

Maya wanted to swim with her, wanted to sink into that quiet blue embrace. She wanted to weave shells and corals through her long hair and lure sailors into the depths, entrancing them with her beauty and her song. She held out her arms, pleading to be taken along as she walked slowly into the water.

The next morning, the sun rose on the gray Ford that still sat in the parking lot above the beach. It was not alone in the lot anymore, sharing the space with two police cruisers, an idle ambulance, and the vehicles of the local Harbor Patrol. Down the path, an anxious knot of people stood around a small beach fire. They would be there for hours more that day — the diving gear, the boats, the radios, the reports, all filtered through the fog of their deepening dread. When the couple finally straggled up the hill to the car, they cursed every step that took them away, each one a commitment to leaving Maya behind, of conceding defeat to the sea.

They would be back as the years went by, many times, in some perverse way taking comfort from that stretch of beach. They didn't understand this in themselves. They didn't know that when they stood there, they listened to the songs that played below their conscious hearing, and, at least temporarily, calmed them.

They also never understood why there were always the most beautiful exotic shells left on the edge of a pool in an inlet down the beach. It was almost as if someone were leaving a gift there for them.

STEVE RUDIS

# Kooshtaka

There is a legend in Southeast Alaska about a half man, half otter creature that roams the woods and streams. Practically no one believes the legend, unless you talk to Zeb Johnson and his girlfriend Lily.

It was a rainy evening just before dark off the coast of Sitka when Zeb and Lily put into a cove in their 36-foot sailboat the Sea Wind, to wait out an approaching storm. Dark clouds floated in from the ocean as the two mariners headed for the safety of the cove near one of the many islands that dot the area.

"This looks like a good spot for the time being," Zeb told Lily.

"Yeah, this should do. But that island over there looks a little ominous to me. Isn't this the area that the old Tlingit Indians say to stay away from…in fear of the Kooshtaka?" Lily asked timidly.

"Oh, you're always imagining things, Lily," said Zeb as he gave her a big hug. "That's just a legend. There's no such thing as a half man, half otter. Let's get something to eat."

After eating a light supper and washing the dishes, the two snuggled into their bunk for a good night's sleep. It wasn't long before they heard a thump toward the bow of the boat.

"What's that?" said Lily as she grabbed Zeb around the neck and the two sat up in bed.

"I don't know. We better go check," Zeb answered.

The two slipped out of their bunk and walked out onto the bow of the boat, carrying high-powered flashlights. They scanned the water through the darkness for a few seconds before Lily's light illuminated a long, narrow, dark form floating in the water. At first she and Zeb thought it was a log. The form began to move, then it turned over, showing it had fangs — as long as a man's fingers — and large red glowing eyes.

Lily screamed. "What is it, Zeb?"

The two stood clutching each other too petrified to move as the creature turned on its belly and swam away. Zeb and Lily slept little that night as they huddled together awaiting sunup.

As they sailed away the next morning, Zeb looked at Lily and said, "Maybe those old Tlingits were right after all."

GALE TRUETT RICHARDSON

# Child of the Stars

Meggie stood completely still in her backyard. White snowflakes shimmered into a misty fluid image. Within seconds the image became a huge fatherly bear standing on its back legs and waving his paw. She shoved her cap higher on her head and gazed her way up to the bear's eyes. As if reading her mind, the bear got down on all fours. His warm, luminous, wise eyes held her in trance.

Meggie gazed at moonlight glistening on his fur and shivered with excitement. Her instinct was to get her mother to share this miracle, but there didn't seem to be enough time. The polar bear was in a hurry and wanted her to go with him.

The bear spoke in thoughts that came complete, not word-by-word. Meggie loved this. It reminded her of her spiritual home where it didn't require effort to speak one's thoughts and feelings. She nodded assent. When he kneeled down, she held onto his fur and pulled her long, lanky body onto his back. Her mind raced.

"What is your name?" she finally asked in the slow, deliberate language of Earth.

"Polaris," the bear replied. "I am a polar bear."

Despite his huge size, Polaris laughed a cute laugh that seemed to Meggie more human than bear. She snuggled into his fluffy fur. It should be cold, she thought. The air is cold. The snow is cold. Yet his fur isn't cold. But these observations evaporated. She didn't have time to think; they were striding along a freeway of light high above Earth. Within minutes Earth was lost to her sight.

Darkness and space engulfed them. Meggie shivered in fear. Until that moment, she was not aware of how far away her mother was. The only familiar Earth sound was the bell Polaris wore on a leather thong around his neck. It reminded her of something. Slowly it came to her: the bell is like God's voice. A cloud of yearning swept over her.

The bell also reminded her of a home with chimes outside the back door. Not on Earth. A different home she no longer remembered, only longed for. She gasped as the bear neared a star and slowed down.

From a distance, the star was an eddying of teddy-bear-brown and snow white. Meggie felt tremors of anticipation run through Polaris as they drew close.

Polaris telepathed to her: "Meggie, this star is An-On. It is a place where beings come to learn about love."

Polaris paused, realizing physical words weren't enough. He also needed to transmit pictures and feelings to her. "There are seven

major stars called The Seven Sisters." As Polaris said the words, he sent mental picture of seven stars with long flowing hair and big eyes, each a different size and color. He waited for her resonating comprehension, then continued. "These stars will soon unite on Earth with the Seven Brothers of the Great Bear constellation." Here Polaris sent a picture of seven stars in bear shapes. These were also slightly different colors and sizes. "When this happens, Earth

244

will know a freedom in love it has never experienced."

Polaris shook his head wistfully. "I am the Great Bear star called Polaris." Meggie's eyes told him she was confused. "I'm sorry. I know in this body you don't understand. But there is more to you than your physical self, and I speak to your entire Being. On a level humans call a 'sub-conscious,' you do understand and this will be important to you. When you grow up, you will be a part of the greatest era Earth has yet to experience. You are important! Remember this much, Meggie, if you remember nothing else. Remember, only love is important!"

Meggie desperately wanted to ask, "What is a sub-conscious?" but she didn't dare. Polaris had said, "Remember, only love is important." She was pretty sure love and sub-conscious were not the same things. Besides, she knew a little about love from her mother. She frowned, remembering her Dad. Was it love that made him leave them? But Meggie didn't want to be sad. She wanted to see and hear and feel this world.

They walked through the light mist until Polaris stepped off the airway onto the ground. Meggie looked around in surprise. Before her was her earthly home. Her mother was still in the kitchen where Meggie had left her. Puzzled, she glanced at the sky. Even the stars looked the same.

Polaris recognized Meggie's bewilderment. "We've entered the spiritual planes," he explained. "It's like when you play with your dolls, while your mother is at work. You both are in the same world, but in different places and doing different things. In the spiritual world, you exist as well. That's the part you don't remember. While your mom on Earth makes one choice, in another world she may make the opposite choice. Here, on An-On, these decisions fuse to become one choice with many parts."

Meggie understood. It seemed natural and right to her. But her memory was fuzzy. She forgot the language her mom was teaching her and spoke fluently in the spiritual language she used with her fairy friends. "I don't understand," she told Polaris. She impulsively hugged the huge bear.

Polaris leaned carefully into her embrace, then spoke again. "You have a wagon in your Earth backyard."

"Yes," Meggie whispered, remembering the Red Devil partially covered with snow. Chill bumps raced along her arms and into her head.

"The wagon is complete with a handle, wheels, and body."

Meggie nodded, listening hard.

"You experience the wagon as a whole unit with many parts."

Meggie's eyes lit up and bobbed with her entire body. Excitement almost blocked out the incoming understanding. "Be still!" she commanded herself.

Polaris flushed with joy; Meggie's delight was difficult to resist, even for an experienced teacher. He linked with her one-word thought, withdrew a memory for her from the Akashic records, the memory of her mother saying, "You have to speak so we can understand you," and sent it to her.

Meggie sighed, took a deep, exasperated breath. "Be still," she commanded herself again, and the slow, verbal sentence took shape and form. It was no longer the cloud-thought the one-word sentence had been. She began to understand. Thoughts and feelings whirled about her. Without warning, she was overcome with sadness, anger and frustration. They weren't distinct feelings, but sticky shrouds of darkness that pulled and probed at her.

Suddenly a thought cleared. She remembered her dad touching her in places that seemed wrong. Then hurting her. She cried out in remembered pain.

Another thought cleared. Her dad was chasing her mom, trying to hit her. She screamed. Feeling alone and deserted, Meggie remembered a time when she was only two months old. Her mother and father had gone away, leaving her with another woman. The caretaker was nice and showed Meggie pictures of her mom and dad. Then she sped forward to when her parents returned from a place called Saudi Arabia. They were the strangers then. Yet they took her from her stand-in mother. Silent tears rode the soft curves down her cheeks.

These feelings had been present all her life, yet not understood. Memories on Earth only projected the pain, not the reasons for it. Here she connected time, place, people, situations and feelings. She felt overwhelmed yet grateful, as if huge blocks of resentment were lifting from her heart.

Polaris wrapped his neck around her. He made a few more vibrational changes so he could more easily communicate with her. When he spoke, his feelings accompanied his words. Meggie felt them: How can I help this beautiful, sensitive, intelligent, talented child get beyond this?

"Let's go back to the wagon in your backyard," Polaris said. "Your pain is like one spoke of that wheel. Yet your physical body is the entire wheel. The wagon holds your entire being, but you know only the one wheel. As the wheel, you feel every bump of the ground, the hardness of concrete, the sinking of sand and the soft, slippery snow.

Your body is but one wheel of your Spirit, which is the wagon. It enables your Spirit to learn the language of Earth. It protects your Spirit so it is free to experience and learn. From pain you learn that others can and will hurt you. You also learn you can hurt others. When these pieces of knowledge unite in understanding, you gain wisdom. That teaches you love, which changes your world."

Polaris gazed intently, yet gently, at Meggie's frazzled aura. He checked her physical mind and her heart. She'll work it out, Polaris thought, nuzzling her hand to comfort her.

Meggie hardly felt the warmth of Polaris' compassion. Confused and forlorn, she sat down on the ground and tuned in to a new level of herself. She didn't know how she had done this. Nor why. She only knew her brain felt like a wheel trying to get over a rock in the road. No matter how she twisted or turned or jumped, she couldn't seem to get beyond the rock.

Emotions twirled around her again, this time colliding into mixtures of joy and sadness. She felt Polaris' furry cheek against hers. Meggie reached out and slid her arms around as much of his neck as she could, then squeezed her gratefulness into him. Somehow she knew the darkness would disappear.

"What you have just experienced, Meggie, is the union of opposites. Do you know what opposites are?" Polaris asked.

"Apples and oranges." Meggie smiled half-heartedly, afraid of disappointing him.

"Close enough!" Polaris said. "When opposites merge, your Spirit understands the entire concept of your experience. If you feel just the joy, or just the sadness, the concept is distorted. So never fear pain. Ask it what it is teaching you."

Meggie tried hard not to yawn. She couldn't figure out how one could have an apple-orange. She did know one thing: she had learned her mother loved her through the pain of when her dad left.

She yawned again, stretching her body. How strange that I listened so long. On Earth listening makes me feel angry and stubborn. The slow words of Earth run over my mind like a dull hum.

As awareness of her surroundings sharpened, Meggie realized she felt cold, not from conscious thought, but because suddenly, somehow there was a fire blazing before her. She held her hands to the flames, realizing she felt no heat, only comfort. Here on An-On these sensations wrapped into a single feeling that warmed her heart.

From a distance she dimly heard "Meg-gie!"

The familiar voice startled her. It was Mom! She was now in her backyard, staring at her wagon. Meggie felt strangely pulled between physical reality and that vague reality she had just lost. Yet she felt freer.

Faint smells came from the kitchen that started Meggie's tummy gurgling. She ran to the house. After stomping the snow from her boots, she stepped into the kitchen. "I'm here, Mom."

She carefully hung her hat and coat on the peg just inside the door. Polaris floated in and out of her mind as she walked over to the stove.

After Meggie washed her hands, her mother lifted a plate of hamburgers and French fries, then handed it to her. "Please put this on the table for me."

Meggie let the scent sear into her being. She hadn't noticed smells on An-On. Memories twinkled, then disappeared before Meggie could grab hold of them.

"Did you look at the stars while you were playing?" Mom asked absently, turning off the stove.

"Yes," Meggie said, suddenly shy. She walked back to her mother, took her hand and led her to the back door. "I visited that one."

# Behind Great Men

"Annu, where are you going?" asks her mother. "Into the forest," replies Annu as she grabs her quiver with bow, flinging them over her back. She pivots towards the doorway.

"No you're not!" replies her mother.

Princess Annu Lightfeather of the wood elves spins to face her mother. She places fists on narrow boyish hips. "And why not?" she protests. "You've always allowed me to go there!"

Lady Lightfeather stops sweeping the floor to confront her daughter's glaring eyes. "Your father says there is danger in the forest."

"Oh that," Annu shrugs. "Father always speaks of danger." She makes an exaggerated flip of her ponytail that allows the braids to sway across her back.

"Your father says the seers have felt danger near the sacred Stone of Protection. They think the magic in the stone has been weakened by some evil force."

"I've been to the glen more than a hundred times and I've never seen anything more frightening than a skunk," she says waving her hands in defiant frustration.

Holding her broom in one hand, Lady Lightfeather shakes her index finger. "You have lived a fortunate life. During your brief fourteen summers, there has been no breach of our sacred Stone of Protection. But, there is danger beyond the stone, and I hope you never face it."

"I don't know what lies beyond the stone. No one allows me such adventures. Only boys are allowed to go outside our protected forest and they've always returned unharmed. I trust our brave wood elf hunters will keep our treetops safe. I'm going anyway and you can't stop me!"

Lady Lightfeather sighs as Annu unhooks the leather strap to the entryway and steps out into the world.

Preferring to live up high in the safety of tall trees, wood elves are much smaller than their distant cousins, the high elves, who live in the snowcapped mountains to the north. The treetop village bustles with activity. A network of suspension bridges joins tree houses and tree shops in every direction. Many of the olive-skinned elves pause to smile and say good morning to Annu as she walks by. But the young male hunters shy away from her bold eyes, looking up only after she passes to watch her bouncing stride and swaying ponytail.

Annu reaches the edge of the treetop village and lowers herself to the ground by rope vine. She proceeds down a path through cultivated vegetable gardens and orchards. After a short walk, she enters an evergreen rain forest of giant firs, sequoias, hanging vines, and flowering bushes. She walks so lightly that the birds and squirrels continue their chatter as she passes.

This enchanted forest is the ancestral home of her wood elf clan, and her senses come alive when she is here. She feels the collective auras of all the plants and animals around her. Drawing from this natural energy, she feels her psychic power surge. The forest is a living being and Annu's soul is one with the forest. She has the gift, and the villagers say she will be among the shamans.

Using her psychic powers, she feels another wood elf following her. She slows her pace, and whoever is following also slows. She feels no danger. Instead, there is playfulness in the air. Perhaps this playmate is testing her psychic abilities.

When she comes to a curve in the path, she steps to one side and crouches behind a fallen tree. She waits for her fellow wood elf to appear, but he is too clever. She feels his presence just beyond view. He also has stopped. Her eyes narrow as she focuses. She has felt his aura before but can't identify him.

Closing her eyes, she prepares herself to use a secret talent that she has never revealed, because some villagers would call her a witch, and they burn witches. Never understanding the fine line between psychic seers and magical witchcraft, she will not let silly superstitions stop her. In deep meditation, she begins to liberate her conscious being from her physical self. Her free spirit wrestles with the awkward sensation of weightless separation, feeling her mind's eye rise above her body, allowing her spirit to hover and adjust to its new freedom, and looking down upon herself, confirming her new perspective.

Her detached sight floats down the path and peers around a bush to see Thor Tallbear hiding behind a tree. With the shock of seeing her future husband, her psychic abilities suddenly stop. Instantly her spirit draws back into her flesh. Her bodily sensations return to a feeling of revulsion. Wavering, she nearly faints, but quickly regains control of her body.

With mixed emotions, Annu thinks of Lady Spinshire. She is the matchmaker of the village and she has already announced that the two shall wed. Annu should be happy. Thor is a strong athletic wood elf of seventeen summers, with a full head of black wavy hair, well-pointed ears, and bulging biceps. He is the best and the brightest of the young wood elf hunters.

Annu's father is Chief Lightfeather, head of the warrior's council. After they are married, Thor will become next in line to become chief of the village. Thor is handsome enough — at four foot ten, he is one of the tallest — but mating and making babies is not what Annu dreams of, at least not yet. Feeling trapped, she sighs. There seems to be no escaping her fate. She dreams of far away lands, evil foes and untold fortunes.

Crouching behind the fallen tree, she ponders what trick she might play on Thor, when another presence enters into her psychic range, chilling her. Blood drains from her face and she turns ghostly white. She has never felt such danger. On the edge of panic, she hesitates, her mind racing. This dangerous beast moves rapidly as a wolf on a scent.

Gathering her thoughts quickly like a cat that senses an approaching dog, she springs onto the path, ducking low, looking in every direction. She must warn Thor. Staying in the shadows, she runs swiftly, silently towards him.

She comes upon Thor with such swiftness that he jumps with fright. "How did you find me?" he protests with a startled smile.

"Quiet! There is danger!" she snaps sternly, gesturing for him to get down.

But Thor stands boldly. "What has spooked my little wife to be?" he laughs. "There is nothing to fear in this forest, or have you forgotten about the magic stone?"

"The magic has failed!" she says with urgency. "Get down!"

"Oh it has, has it?" He continues to mock her. "And why would it pick this day to fail?"

Suddenly there is the crashing sound of a massive creature charging through the forest. Thor freezes as Annu pulls him down by his tunic.

"What's that?" whispers Thor in terror.

"It has our scent!" says Annu as she puts a knee to the ground and readies an arrow to her bow.

Baritone laughter rumbles from the shadows. "Hmm, me smell elf."

Thor screams, "Run!" as he jumps to his feet and darts like a terrified rabbit down the path. The monster is quicker, and Thor gets only a few yards when a three-hundred-pound ogre with green leathery pigskin steps out to block his way. The eight-foot monster has the face of a warthog, covered with hairy moles, dark blemishes and a flared pig nose. Two-inch tusks overlap fangs, making the perfect weapon for tearing off the arms and legs of scrawny elves.

Thinking her future husband might not be so brave, Annu lets her arrow fly and it strikes the ogre in the center of his chest. However, the arrow barely penetrates the thick hide, stopping at the hard bone of the sternum. Unfazed, the ogre simply pulls it out and tosses it away.

"Me have little elf for supper!" says the ogre leaping towards Thor, who stumbles backwards as the ogre grabs him by the neck and picks him off the ground. With feet dangling, Thor is shaken and choked by the ogre. He is unable to breathe, and the pain paralyzes him.

Annu knows that Thor's neck is about to snap like a twig. Something inside her awakens. A dormant power deep within her soul wells up and takes control. Time stands still as energy floods into her expanding mind. She feels she is about to explode when a surge of psychic energy blasts from her third-eye chakra. The unseen force stuns the ogre like a war hammer striking his forehead. He drops Thor and staggers back. In dazed confusion, the ogre blinks his eyes and shakes his head. Thor struggles to his feet, gasping for breath.

"Draw your dagger!" screams Annu. "Draw your dagger!"

Moments pass as the ogre and Thor gawk at each other. Finally Thor comes to his senses and draws his three-foot dagger with a sharp point for stabbing. The ogre rubs his eyes and begins to focus. Thor hesitates as red eyes stare down at him.

Then the ogre jumps forward, reaching for Thor. Again Annu releases a wave of psychic energy, and again the ogre is stunned backwards.

"Now!" she screams.

Thor stabs his blade up into the soft underbelly of the huge monster, but the dagger fails to penetrate. Bracing his feet and using both hands, he shoves the blade hard. Blood gushes as it rips through tough hide and sinks into soft gut. Still stunned, the ogre can only stand in disbelief. Thor stabs repeatedly, twisting his blade until the monster's belly spills out. Thor steps back as the ogre clutches his exposed guts, doubles over and falls to the ground. One last stab to the monster's jugular and the two elves watch as the ogre thrashes about, drowning in his own blood.

Thor turns to Annu. "I've killed an ogre!" he says, apparently amazed at himself.

"Yes, you did," says Annu, wondering if Thor suspects she used magic.

"I really did it!"

"I know, I saw."

He turns to look back at his trophy. "No wood elf has ever killed an ogre alone! That makes me the greatest warrior of all time!"

"Yes you are, and you saved my life," she says preferring not to reveal her witching ways.

Like an excited little boy, Thor turns back to Annu. "I did it, didn't I? I saved you!"

Annu nods thoughtfully, relieved that he seems to know nothing of her newfound power.

Thor breathes deeply, expanding his chest. "Come, my bride, we must go back to the village and boast of my heroism!"

Forcing a smile, Annu sighs and takes Thor by the arm, "Perhaps you should also warn them that the stone has been breached." With new confidence and nothing to fear, her thoughts drift beyond the Stone of Protection. She dreams of far away lands, evil foes and untold fortunes.

# The End

SHIRLEY MATHIS

It came without warning,
A barrier I could not penetrate.
With eyes wide open
I surveyed the world
And realms of fantasy,
Drank in the beauty,
Wallowed in the dirty.

All of it I experienced with glee.
I did not think about the end.
Alas it came to be.
The final page,
The words, "The End."
I did not want to comprehend.

A light came on within my brain,
    It said:
"Open the book and start again."

# Contributors

DONNA ANDERSON has been writing for many years. She writes children's books and mystery novels, but the thing that is getting published is her newspaper writing. Donna writes a monthly column about her hometown, Hansville, Washington. Anderson also writes essays and articles for magazines. "I am currently writing a book about Bridge Groups," (the card game) she says, "but my favorite writing is short stories."

SHERRY BENIC is an artist and writer who has made Washington her adopted home. She pays her mortgage as an educator, and feeds her soul through her art and writing. Sherry's poetry and illustrations appeared in *The Sun Never Rises — A Rainthology*. "I live with a dog and cat who have inspired me to live in the moment," she says. Her hobbies and interests include thinking about gardening, spoiling her grandchildren, and reading English mysteries.

CHARLIE BROUGH and his wife Grace once owned a twenty-pound cat named Rat. While living at Ocean Shores WA, Rat somehow fell down a brick chimney into the grating of a fireplace. Charlie has put into words Rat's confinement. "Rat tells about his narrow escape with death and his happiness in being reunited with his mistress," says Brough. This author has written many short stories and his just-published historical novel, *Thank God For Pigs*.

J. R. CARLSEN, a Baby-Boomer from Chicago, probably inherited her desire to travel from her European ancestors. A yearning to trace her heritage and the urging by another author and dear friend led her to a creative writing class — and the spark was fanned. Admiration for the late Erma Bombeck's writing style triggered plans to share witty stories about family with future generations. Along the way, her creativity varied from writing facts (articles for various church, school and club activities, textbooks, resumes, etc.) to writing her first fiction short story, "Clock Shop." E-mail your comments to her at jrcarlsen@aol.com.

JULIA COUSINEAU has had several short stories and essays published in various literary magazines. Three of her stories and one essay appeared in a previous anthology, *The Sun Never Rises — A Rainthology*. In the past few years Julia has had a one-act play produced through the South Sound Playwrights Festival and is currently writing a newspaper column titled, "Humor Me!" Besides her day job, she instructs Personal Enrichment classes at Tacoma Community College in all forms of writing. Her best writing advice: Never say you've put a work to bed unless you're sure it won't sleepwalk!

NANCY COVERT, a former journalist-turned-freelance writer, divides her time between a variety of writing-oriented activities including poetry, short stories, and travel articles, as well as reading stories to her grandchildren. Originally from Pennsylvania, she makes her home in Steilacoom, the oldest incorporated community in Pierce County where she is actively involved in a variety of civic organizations and activities.

P. JUNE DIEHL has published numerous nonfiction articles during the past several years. A former public school teacher, she has worked in the computer field for the past twenty years, many of them as a technical writer. Online, she works as an editor, writing coach, and teacher in the craft of writing. She currently has five ongoing fiction series, and is the editor of *Writer's Crossing*. Her chapbook *Dragon Words: Assorted Poems* is currently available. You can visit her at: http://clik.to/iwriteforyou.

JACQUELINE DOCK lived in Iowa, but met her husband J. Oden while clamming at the Washington coast. Since their marriage, they have lived in Illinois, Germany, Texas and now Steilacoom WA. Jackie has published in the Steilacoom Historical Museum's quarterly magazine, the *Subscript*, Lakewood Historic Society's *Clock Tower*, and Audobon's *Toyhee*. Her photographs have been published in the *Lakewood Journal* and the *Tacoma News Tribune*.

J. ODEN DOCK hopes that his children's story helps youngsters realize they already are superior to adults in these ways: children are more observant and more imaginative. "Many authors' stories encourage children to believe that in order to be equal to an adult they need magic rings or the power of wizards." J.O. Dock's other published works have appeared in *Toyhee*, *The Ranger*, *The Clock Tower* and *The Sun Never Rises*.

VAL DUMOND has been writing most of her life, professionally since 1980 — articles, advertising copy, and books. Her published work includes *Grammar For Grownups*, *Elements of Nonsexist Usage*, *Doin' the Puyallup*, *Mush On and Smile — Klondike Kate, Queen of the Yukon*, and *Just Words* (soon to be released). As facilitator of the Writers Roundtable in Tacoma, she works with authors to help them publish. She edited the group's first anthology, *The Sun Never Rises*, and compiled the works of *Dream Makers* and nudged it into print.

PETER FENTON was born and raised in Spokane and has lived in Tacoma WA for more than twenty-five years. After several years of writing and publishing technical documents for companies such as Boeing and Microsoft, Fenton decided to focus on creative writing. Recently he completed his first fantasy novel, *Wizards Born*. "While exploring publication, I'm writing short stories," he says.

MATTHEW A. GERACI
> I write to move, for as a river moves, my hand is moved.
> As the rains fill the stream, my heart is filled.
> Though the rain falls, my hand is moved.
> Though the ground swallows the rain.
> This is why I write, that thy words may fall upon others' hearts.

JEAN HANNAN's grandmother urged her to write as a child. Hannan's first published work was her grandfather's obituary. She wrote stories, poems, articles and columns throughout school and college and while raising four children. Then she wrote stories for adults and professional articles for Michigan State University. At 50 she moved to "the other Washington" to enjoy new adventures to write about: mountain horsepacking, hiking, running rivers, golf and skiing. Among Hannan's published work are: *A View of the Sky*, *A Stitch in Time*, *Selway Retreat*, *The Last Sail*, *Not Writing 500 Words*, *Centennial Biography*, and *Remembering Larry*. She has received gold and silver awards for poetry anthologies. "All this," she says, "from a sense of humor and quality eavesdropping."

ROBERT HARTLE is a Tacoma WA poet currently working on a poetry handbook for children. He and his beautiful wife Kari have two wonderful sons, Ethan and Austin, for whom Hartle is writing a children's series. Hartle works at Stadium High School to support his poetry habit.

NADINE McKEE HENRY has been writing most of her life. She has written columns for newspapers and *National Garden* magazine. She has written stories and character pieces for several periodicals, including *Leather Neck* and *Sunset Magazine*. A Master Gardener for 20 years, Henry co-authored "Selected Rhododendron Glossary and Botanical Terms" and "Getting the Most For Your Garden." She has penned the *Gourmet Gardeners Handbook* and two novels, *Crossing Heirs* and *Pigtails in the Wind*. Henry has traveled to all seven continents, including the Antarctic (her most recent trek).

JANELLE MERAZ HOOPER is a writer from Oklahoma with a Hispanic background. Her first novel, *A Three-Turtle Summer*, was published in September 2002. Her second, *Devil's Rope: The Indianhead Diaries*, is due to be published in 2003. She has been a contributing writer to *The Northwest Guardian Newspaper* as well as other newspapers, magazines, books, and the Internet. Born and raised in Oklahoma, she now lives near Seattle with her husband. Contact Janelle at hooperdj@nwrain.com.

JULIE JENNINGS has had an avid interest in writing since she was nine. She teaches writing and facilitates a course at WVU. A native of Tacoma WA, Jennings published three stories online last year. Her current love is her novel, *Villa Manchez*. She's written for the Cuyamaca College newspaper and participated in writing for the Historical Society in Spring Valley CA, along with writing newsletters for school and church, and her own Pearls Newsletter online. A member of NAWW and Writers Roundtable, her short story and several poems appeared in *The Sun Never Rises — A Rainthology*. Check out: jrjennings.net/writing/

PETER JENNINGS writes poetry when he's not practicing on his guitar or writing songs. His favorite sports are soccer and hacky sack (if you consider hacky sacking a sport). He was born in San Diego

CA in 1986 and now lives in Spanaway WA. He plans to publish more of his poems.

PATRICIA LAWTON has traveled to many places, but her heart and soul belong in her native Washington. There she has had the joy of raising and sharing the area with her three children and now grandchildren. Lawton has always loved the power of words, whether poetry, anecdotes — sad or funny — or long sagas. "Life with all it has to offer gives me unlimited material to write about," she says. "The wonderful group, the Writers Roundtable, encourages me free rein."

ALINE LESAGE, born and raised in Québec City, Canada, of a French father and Irish mother, attended Ottawa University and established herself as an English-French translator. An avid traveler, she later worked as a French teacher in Jamaica where she developed a strong and lasting connection. She recently moved to the Northwest where writing has become her main occupation. Lesage's ongoing work includes a biographical novel recounting the fates of her Québécois kinswomen over four generations. She says, "*On Folly Road* is a genuine snapshot of my Caribbean experience."

TOM MARTIN writes mostly ghastly, dark fiction, but gets his nonfiction books published. Tom's books include *Contingency Cannibalism*, which he wrote as "Shiguro Takada," and *Behind Prison Walls*, which details the more regular but sinister aspects of prison life. When not writing about prisons, living dead, cannibals, murderers, and humor, he might work in a prison, or teaching various subjects to state employees on surviving harsh realities.

SHIRLEY MATHIS was fifty years old when she decided to become a serious writer. Twenty years later her goal is to record her adventures as a mother of five, especially the events related to being the mother of a son murdered at age twenty-one. She has doodled with poetry since high school childhood years in Canada where the family lived in many small towns, including a logging camp at Crow's Nest in British Columbia. "I particularly enjoy writing memoir, recalling long forgotten adventures, and conceiving stories with pen and paper."

CALUNA MITCHELL lives in the Puget Sound basin, where beauty combines with precipitation to inspire reading and writing. "I am rediscovering a writing talent uncovered by a student teacher, Mr. Ogden, who focused on my strengths and helped me find ways to overcome the undiagnosed disorders," she says. "With the help of a companion computer and spellcheck, friends, and a collective known as the Writers Roundtable, I am able to compensate for my learning disabilities."

SHANNON O'DONNELL told her third grade teacher, "My brother died," and got instant sympathy and prayers from her classmates. "When my parents confronted me five days later, I compounded the lie, claiming it was a story told by one of my fifty classmates," she says. O'Donnell lives in Tacoma and writes poetry, essays, and short stories. Her work as a prison chaplain is enriched by the tales she hears and the ones she tells. She swaps stories about writing with her brother who has not yet died.

CHARLOTTE RICHARDS was a Civil Service historian whose air base histories were selected as the best in two Air Force commands. She began writing on an Ohio farm and says, "Our farmhouse attic was a treasure trove of old books which inspired me to compose my first effort, a two-page poem, at the age of nine." Since then, Richards' works have appeared in such publications as *Reader's Digest, Redbook, Alfred Hitchcock's Mystery Magazine,* and *Writers' Journal.* In addition to winning numerous writing contests, she has edited and published books for other authors, including several anthologies for a Tacoma WA writers' group.

GALE TRUET RICHARDSON, born in Georgia, traveled the United States and became used to not having the same roof over her head. When she moved to Washington, she learned not to take the sun for granted. The gray skies prompted many kinds of writing. She has published a book of her poetry and several stories and poems, all coming from insight and intrigue. Richardson is working on two novels and feels "outlawed by the Land of Oz." Her book, *Spirit of the Wall,* is in its tenth year of rewrites. She says, "I write in order to understand Life and Love, so it's a lifetime occupation."

MICHAEL ROBBINS is damned if he knows where inspiration comes from. "What I do know is there are a lot of things that anger me, and when I get on a tangent I'll ride it full bullocks," he says. "I ain't articulate, and writing has always come naturally." Robbins claims to be the youngest of six hooligans, a diabetic for most of his years, and a confirmed liberal. His writing credits range from packages for the family at holidays to fiction, essays and contributions to two other anthologies. He also has a beef "with der state of Washington."

STEVE RUDIS is a real-life adventurer who likes to share his experiences with readers. Beginning in the 1970s, he did commercial fishing off the coast of Alaska, worked at logging camps in Southeast Alaska, worked on the trans-Alaska oil pipeline, and more. "The characters I have met and write about make up the last American frontier," he says. Rudis recently completed *Travels of an Alaskan Tramp*, a book about his years in Alaska.

KIM RYAN lives in Tacoma with her two sons, two cats, and the occasional borrowed teenager. She graduated the Evergreen State College in 1990 with a bachelor degree in psychology/sociology, and works full time as credit and collection analyst in the transportation industry. "I enjoy sculpting and music as well as writing," she says. "With my spare time (?) I love to read — fantasy and horror stories most of all." Ryan grew up with her nose in a book and has decided it's time to get her own stories out there!

DAN SLOAN, an electrical engineer for thirty-five years, has written many operators' manuals for equipment he installed. Three years ago he began his foray into the realm of non-technical writing with a short story, "The Cure," written as an entry into a Halloween horror story contest. Since then he's been producing more wry stories. "Googly Time," a move into poetry, is a tone poem inspired by Lewis Carroll's "Jaberwocky."

JAMES FRANCIS SMITH harbored a desire to write historical novels following a lengthy career in finance. He currently is working on book two of the *Life And Times of The O'Donnells*, a novel about growing up Irish in Philadelphia. His narratives in this anthology demonstrate his ability to develop short stories as well. Smith previously published the highly acclaimed *Path to a Successful Retirement*.

JODI SULLIVAN, a native Seattleite and the daughter of an Air Force career man, has climbed rubber trees in Bermuda's Botanical Gardens and picked pine nuts in the mountains outside Reno NV. Later the love of travel took her on adventures of her own and into a career as a travel agent. "A journal, which I kept on a trip to Ireland, inspired my desire to write more," she says. Her published works include poetry, letters to local newspapers, a number of travel articles in trade publications and two short stories in this anthology. Sullivan resides in Tacoma WA, where she is working on two books.

DAVID SWEET is a poet who keeps his hand in a variety of activities: nature, life and the Universe, working with people, Life Coaching, sales and marketing training, and personal growth. He says, "I love to work with my hands." As a coach and lecturer, he helps others discover who they are. He recently published his book of poems, plays, tales and short stories, *Stones Winds and Life*, and is completing his second (untitled) book. Visit www.Sweetpoetry.com or contact him at Sweetpoetry@mindspring.com. "Who defines you?" he wants you to ask yourself.

BARBARA J. WYATT is an adventurer and business executive who incorporates her travel experiences and explorations into her writing. "Ain't No Alabama Hillbilly" was written early one summer morning on the shores of Lake Martin. She and her family spent several weeks traveling throughout Alabama and Georgia studying the history of the South. "It's a puzzle where this macabre story came from," she says. "I have a nephew, Andy, who is a talented and delightful man, and I know Lake Martin and its wildlife. I borrowed Andy's name and the Lake Martin wildlife, and…this tale emerged." Wyatt is married to an absolutely fascinating man.

# Acknowledgements

You are reading a book put together through the efforts of many people — a kind of committee project. Thirty-three writers contributed their work to make up the text. A reading/editing committee produced the final stories and poems for compilation. The entire Writers Roundtable selected the opening and closing poems and chose the cover illustration from a variety of entries. A marketing committee plans sales and distribution. And the writers themselves invest in the printing costs. Here are the names of a few of those hard workers:

Tom Martin came up with the original concept for this book project and continued to provide the steam to make it happen.

Dan Sloan headed the Production Committee. He also took the photograph that was selected for the cover.

Charles Kuhn heads the Marketing Committee.

Gale Truett Richardson drew the charming child riding a bear that accompanies her story that begins on Page 243.

Aline LeSage drew the house that accompanies her story on Page 107.

Sherry Benic contributed the rest of the illustrations, including the distinctive design of the Section Pages.

Mark Ashley, of SandsCostner & Associates, Tacoma, WA, designed the beautiful cover.

Val Dumond and Muddy Puddle Press contributed the formatting and printing of this volume.

Every one of the thirty-three authors is involved in the publishing, promoting and marketing of Dream Makers.

To them and to all who contributed to the producing of this book, a huge

## Thank You

# Index

# WRITE YOUR STORY HERE:

# For Additional Copies

# *Dream Makers*

## *Stories That Won't Put You To Sleep*

## Don't let go. . .

of your copy of this collection of short stories and poems — especially selected work by authors of the Writers Roundtable.

## Order more copies. . .

for your friends. Help them discover the wide variety of stories that won't put you to sleep!

■■■■■■■■■■■■■■■■■■■■■■■■■■■■■■■■■■■■■■■■■■■■

Please send me _____ copies of DREAM MAKERS. Enclosed is a check or money order for $18.95 ($14.95 per book, plus $4 S&H. In Washington, add $1.26 tax.) Mail to:
**Muddy Puddle Press, P O Box 97124, Tacoma, WA 98497**

NAME _____

ADDRESS _____

PHONE (_____)_____

## Information: 253-582-5453